SECRETS OF COMMUNICATION MASTERY

18 LASER-FOCUSED TACTICS TO COMMUNICATE MORE EFFECTIVELY

Mike Agugliaro

ISBN-13: 978-1515290827
ISBN-10: 1515290824

CONTENTS

INTRODUCTION

As a business owner or manager, you have certain expectations. For example, you have expectations about how your team will operate and you have expectations about the standards they achieve in their work. Have you ever been surprised or disappointed when the outcome of their work was different than your expectations?

It doesn't just happen with employees, does it? Perhaps you've faced the same problem with vendors: you have an expectation that they'll deliver something and the outcome turns out to be different. Maybe they delivered too much or two little or the invoice was not what you were expecting.

It also happens with customers, too: You do the work you were hired to do, only to encounter some surprise at the very end because the customer's expectations were different than the outcome. Maybe they were expecting a different price or didn't understand that the project would take as long as it did.

It happens outside of work as well: perhaps our spouse has an expectation that we'll be home in time for supper but we end up running late with a customer. The outcome, of course, is conflict when we finally do get home. Or perhaps we set an expectation with a teenage child that they get home at a certain time on Friday night… and sometimes the outcome ends up being very different.

Expectations and outcomes… We face them every day. We set expectations and we observe outcomes constantly through each day. When they align, everything is good. But the reality is: they don't always align.

We know what happens when expectations and outcomes don't align: There is usually some negative feeling – perhaps disappointment, anger, resentment, or even verbalized conflict.

Why is it that our expectations don't always align with the outcomes? Certainly there might be extenuating factors that influence an outcome: for example, our team might be expected to complete a job in one day and they take two days because there was a delay on a key part. Or perhaps our teenage child didn't get home in time because they accompanied a friend to the hospital during an emergency. Those are extenuating circumstances, and they happen from time to time.

But more often than not, expectations and outcomes do not always match up because of **communication**.

Our lives are all about communication: We communicate with others for a number of reasons, such as: to get information, to direct others, to

5

share our opinion, to help, to set expectations, and more. Nearly every moment that you're with someone else, you're communicating with them (sometimes verbally, sometimes not). So much of what we do is communication.

However, communication is a very complex process (much more complex than most people realize), which is why we so often set an expectation but see a different outcome.

Although there are occasionally extenuating circumstances for the difference between expectations and outcomes, we should first look to our own communication to help us bridge the gap between our expectations and the outcomes we get as a result.

In this book I will share with you several powerful strategies you need to become proficient at communication. You'll discover just how complex communication is and you'll read about strategies to communicate more effectively, no matter what the situation.

When you master your communication, you will discover that you have an amazing previously untapped power at your disposal to help you get whatever you want in business… and even in life!

- Your team will get more work done and more of it will be aligned with your vision for your company
- Your vendors will start delivering exactly what you want
- Your customers will be happier because they'll better understand what you intend to deliver
- Even your family life will improve because you'll communicate more effectively with your spouse and children.

In my book *The Secrets Of Business Mastery*, I revealed the twelve areas of business that you need to master and transform in order to help you grow your service business, gain control of your life and wealth, and dominate your market. The book you're reading right now (which can be read before, after, or at the same time as *The Secrets Of Business Mastery*) explains how communication plugs into each area of your life and business and helps you set better expectations and achieve better outcomes. You should also read my second book, *Secrets of Leadership Mastery*, which talks about how to develop a high performing team and build a culture that serves your customers. All three of these books (*The Secrets Of Business Mastery*, *Secrets of Leadership Mastery*, and this book, *Secrets Of Communication Mastery*) work together to help you master your business and your team, and raise your business to a higher level.

A Few Important Notes About The Book

As you'll soon discover, communication can be delivered in different ways: ideas are sometimes communicated through spoken word and sometimes communicated through written word. Regardless of how you communicate, the principles are the same. So in this book I'll generally use terms like "speak" and "listen" but they apply equally well to the written word. Occasionally, if I'm talking about a written communication specifically, I'll use words like "write" (instead of "speak") and "read" (instead of "listen"), but in general I'll use the speak/listen terminology for consistency.

I've made this book as practical as possible by including *Take Action!* sections at the end of each chapter. Use those sections to identify actions you need to stop doing, keep doing, or start doing, to set dates around those actions, and to find people to help you (for delegation or accountability). Filling out each *Take Action!* section will turn this book from passive information into active, business-improving implementation.

LASER-FOCUSED TACTIC #1: UNLOCKING THE MYSTERY OF COMMUNICATION

Your day is filled with setting expectations and observing the outcome. It doesn't matter if you're doing this with employees, vendors, customers, family, friends, or the barista at Starbucks… Your entire day is filled with expectations and outcomes.

And the way you set those expectations is through communication. In fact, it's impossible to set expectations in any other way. Communication is the only way that you share what you think, feel, and want.

Communication is vital to your business. Communication is the system by which you set expectations, build relationships, and serve your employees and customers.

When I say "communication" most people think of it as the words we speak. But communication is so much more complex than that. Communication is made up of several components:

- The words we use
- The words we don't use!
- The tone of our voice
- The speed we deliver those words
- Our body language (in fact, this can often say more than our words will say!)
- The environment in which we're communicating
- The medium we're using to communicate (face-to-face, telephone, email, text, etc.)
- The ability of the listener to understand

Consider this very simple example: Imagine that you are ordering coffee at a coffee shop…

- The words you use would probably be "I'd like a cup of coffee". That makes the most sense but even that is not enough. What size? Do you like light roast or dark roast? Do you want milk or sugar? The words you use need to be clear and specific.
- The words you don't use are just as important: If you said: "Give me cup of coffee right now", you may end up with a very difference

experience at the coffee shop. Or, if you asked for a mug of coffee instead of a cup, you might end up with a ceramic mug of coffee when you were hoping for a coffee to go.

- Your tone will also have an effect. Try saying "I'd like a cup of coffee" in different ways – as a question, as a loud and direct command, as a statement, as a whisper, etc. Even though you're using the same words, each one of these conveys an entirely different meaning.

- The speed of your words will also play a role on the message. Saying "I'd like a cup of coffee" very quickly sends an urgency, while saying it slowly paints a completely different picture of your message. Sometimes saying something too quickly or too slowly will also impact how well the message is understood.

- Body language will also influence your message (often more than the words you speak). Whether you point aggressively with one finger at the person you're speaking to, or you're relaxed and slouching with your hands in your pockets, or even if you wink at the person while you're talking to them – each of these communicate something different.

- The environment you're communicating in will also impact the understanding as well: If you are in a coffee shop and you ask for coffee, the barista will make the coffee for you; but if you ask for coffee and you're in a convenience store, the cashier will likely point to their coffee pot; and if you're at your office and you ask for coffee, someone might just go to the coffee machine and get you coffee.

- The medium you're using to communicate will also influence how quickly you get your coffee: Face-to-face in a coffee shop will probably get you one coffee. But what if you call a busy employee who is on the road and ask them to pick up coffee? They might be distracted by driving through traffic and think you mean that you will mean that they should pick up coffee for themselves and bill it to the company.

- And, the ability of the listener to understand you will also impact your message. The language they speak and the culture they were raised in will have an impact on whether they understand and how well they'll be able to carry out your request.

As I've broken down the communication process for something as simple as ordering a coffee, you can see just how complex the communication process is! Now consider how the communication process can be even more complex when you're talking about running your service business and giving instructions (sometimes highly technical or very specific instructions) to your team about the work you expect.

Like a machine, communication is complex and, just like a machine, if one of these components doesn't work correctly, the communication machine doesn't work.

Think of communication like an invisible assembly line: It starts in your brain as the idea forms and the idea takes shape through words, tone, and speed. Then it leaves your mouth and the idea takes further shape through your body language. Those words travel through space from your mouth to your listener's ear and they take even more meaning in the environment you're in. Once your idea arrives at the listener's ear, their ability to understand what you have to say changes the shape of the idea even further.

The communication machine takes the idea you have in your mind and tries to rebuild it as closely as possible in your listener's mind. If your communication skills are effective then the idea is the same in your mind and theirs, and ultimately the outcome will be aligned with your expectations. But if too many of the components of the communication machine are not as effective then the idea in your mind will look very different when it is appears in your listener's mind... and the outcome will not be aligned with the expectation.

I'm reminded of a news story I read recently where someone was filming a scene for a movie in a city park. They tweeted that they were "shooting in the park." The words were accurate and innocent. But there is so much more meaning to those words when not understood properly, plus the medium used to communicate the message didn't give a lot of context. The innocent tweet turned into a major event as police locked down nearby buildings.

And when the communication machine doesn't work, expectations don't align with outcomes and that's a problem.

The first step in mastering your communication is to understand the complexity of the process and realize that there are so many different components that gather together to form a single idea and to get that idea from your head into the head of your listener.

It's a mistake to hope that your team understands you perfectly every time. Rather, as a leader, it's your job to understand that communication is a skill that can be practiced and honed, just like any other skill, and the more effective you become at communicating, the better you will become at setting the right expectations. And the resulting outcomes will be more in line with what you want to achieve.

Take Action!

(Add a checkmark beside each one when complete):

__ Stop doing actions (Actions you currently do now but should stop doing)

_____

_____

__ Keep doing actions (Actions you currently do now and should keep doing)

_____

_____

__ Start doing actions (Actions you don't do now but should start doing)

_____

_____

__ Who will do new actions? (Assign the action to yourself or someone else)

_____

_____

__ By when? (When will these actions be complete?)

_____

_____

LASER-FOCUSED TACTIC #2: THE POWER OF CONTEXT

"Hit me."

Those words have very different outcomes if you're at the blackjack table or if you're in the boxing ring. (And if you're at the blackjack table, you don't want to have the same outcome as you'd have if you were in the boxing ring!)

Why is it that when you're sitting at the blackjack table, someone doesn't reach across and punch you in the face?

It has to do with something called "context". Context is the information and circumstances surrounding a specific piece of information. In the example above, "hit me" is the piece of information, while the context is whether you are sitting at a blackjack table or you are squaring off against an opponent in a boxing ring.

In the previous chapter I revealed many of the components that make up the communication process. Each one of those components work together to shape the idea you have in your mind and rebuild it as closely as possible in your listener's mind.

Each of those components is influenced by the context that the communication takes place in. To use the example from the previous chapter, if you asked for coffee and were standing near a coffee machine, the proximity of the coffee machine would suggest that you wanted coffee from that machine. Or, if you had a conversation earlier with someone about Starbucks and then later in the day you asked them for coffee, they will probably go to Starbucks to get it.

Context includes the conversations and ideas that led up to the communication, it includes the environment you're in right now, and it also includes the background of the listener.

Remember the example of the tweet about shooting in the park? There was no context for that tweet so people misunderstood the word "shooting" and reacted accordingly.

In your business, context may include anything from the instructions you gave an employee earlier in the day to the way they view you as the leader. You can give the same instruction to two people and receive two very different outcomes because of context: one employee might have the context that you are a competent leader who knows exactly what to do because they've seen you do the same thing before; another employee might have just joined your team from another company where the leader only gave suggestions – not direction. That second employee's context is very different than the first and they may choose not to follow your instructions. Before you communicate anything awareness of the context that your communication will be received in is essential.

Context is like the foundation of a house. The house is built on the foundation and takes its shape, and a strong foundation will ensure a sturdy, long-lasting house.

The right context will ensure that many of the components of the communication process will be understood correctly. In fact, context can even help to overcome problems with many of the components. Even if your words aren't as clear as they need to be, or even if your listener doesn't fully understand what you are trying to say, the context can help.

If you want to increase the likelihood that your communication connects with your audience, make sure the context is established before the communication begins.

For example:

- If you want to have open communication where ideas are shared and everyone collaborates on a solution, then you want to establish a meeting where people are in a circle and someone is appointed as a facilitator and everyone is encouraged to share. You might say something like, "I want to get all of your ideas…"
- If you want to give a very specific directive where you provide instruction and your team follows through on those instructions, then you need to gather everyone together and explain why they are gathered before you start giving directions. You might say something like, "I have some very specific step-by-step instructions that need to be followed in order…"

In written communication, context is perhaps more important because the person isn't there to hear you or ask questions – they are in a completely separate environment when they read your communication. So establishing the context before you give your communication is important. For example, you might say, "Earlier today we spoke about the importance of greeting the customer in a specific way. In this email, I want to give you the script that I'd like you to say when you greet the customer…"

See how that one sentence set the context? If you just gave them the script without establishing the context you might not get the same outcome as you would by first establishing the context.

Before you make any communication – whether spoken or written – identify the context that the communication will be delivered in. Ask yourself:

- What will the listener/reader have encountered prior to receiving this communication?
- Where will the listener/reader receive this communication?
- What might the listener/reader be thinking about when they receive this communication?

Thinking proactively about your listener's context will help you communicate more effectively.

Take Action!

___ Stop doing actions (Actions you currently do now but should stop doing)

_____

_____

___ Keep doing actions (Actions you currently do now and should keep doing)

_____

_____

___ Start doing actions (Actions you don't do now but should start doing)

_____

_____

__ Who will do new actions? (Assign the action to yourself or someone else)

_____

_____

__ By when? (When will these actions be complete?)

_____

_____

LASER-FOCUSED TACTIC #3: HOW TO READ PEOPLE'S MINDS

As you read earlier, communication is a complex process – a machine – that tries to recreate our idea in our listener's mind. The closer we get to exactly replicating that idea, the better outcomes we'll get from whatever we're trying to communicate.

There are many factors that determine how we communicate an idea, from the words we say to the context we communicate in. But a key factor that influences whether someone understands or not is impacted by the listener themselves.

When we get information – whether by listening or reading – we analyze and modify it in our mind, relative to the ideas and thoughts that we already have. Each person has different experiences, which means that when a person receives a message, it is interpreted in that person's preferred wording and language.

Our understanding is mainly influenced by six filters.

1. Language
2. Meta Programs
3. Belief Systems
4. Values
5. Memories
6. Decisions

Each of these filters can influence how effective your communication is! Let's take a deeper look into these filters that affect our understanding.

Language

Language helps us recognize words based on our ability to understand them, and our previous experience using those words. Our usage and understanding of words are decisive in interpreting a message. When you speak to someone, be mindful of the words you use.

For your team, be aware that some words might hold more meaning than others. This will be influenced by their training and experience in the industry, as well as their own background, upbringing, and previous employment.

For example, if a new employee joins your team and came from a company where coarse joking was accepted, their language will sound very different and should be addressed before they are sent off to a customer's house to represent your company.

Another language factor to be aware of is industry acronyms and jargon, and this could complicate communication with customers. Have you ever walked into a restaurant to order wine and the server gave you a list of wines that sounded like several made-up words strung together? Or have you ever brought your car into be repaired and the mechanic told you what the problem was but it meant absolutely nothing to you?

The exact same thing happens in the home service industry as well. For example, if you're an electrician and you tell a customer that you have 12-guage in your truck, they might wonder why you brought a shotgun to the job! This is a potential problem in every tradeline and industry since each one has its own lingo, jargon, and acronyms. It's okay to use those terms when you are communicating with other professionals but watch those words when communicating with customers.

Another component of language is empowering versus disempowering words. Without realizing it, we adopt words into our vocabulary that can disempower those we're communicating with. As a leader, you don't want to disempower your team but you may be doing so without realizing it.

For example, you might tell you team "Here's the job we have assigned today. I can't see how we're going to get this done in the time allotted but that's the assignment." Without realizing it, you're setting your team's expectations for failure. A simple change would be: "Here's our job for the day. Although time is short, I know we can pull together and get it done. I'd like to hear some ideas about how we can work more effectively in the time available." See the difference? The first example disempowered your team while the second example empowered them.

And this is just one example of the many times throughout the day that our word choice can empower or disempower our teams. Carefully assess the words you say (and have someone listen to you and give you feedback later) to help communicate in a more empowering way.

Meta Programs

This is a complicated word for a very high-level concept: Meta programs are a set of thought and behavior patterns that operate beyond the conscious level. These patterns control one's attention during conversation, habitual linguistic patterns, and body language.

Think of a meta program as the DNA of your communication. It combines together all the different components of your communication that you don't even realize you're doing while you're communicating.

Knowing your own meta program can help you make changes to communicate more effectively. For example, if you know that you come across as pretty aggressive and demanding because of your tone and posture then you can consciously work at easing up a little bit when you want to communicate differently.

And, knowing someone else's meta programs, especially in a work environment, will help you to predict their behavior and actions better. This will help you communicate in a way that they can accurately interpret the information.

Note: Be careful not to confuse someone's meta program with racial or gender profiling. Although racial background and gender can influence someone's meta program, it is far from the only factor.

Values

Values are the things we hold as being more important than anything else in life. Values drive us. Our values are what get us out of bed in the morning and our values determine what actions we take.

If someone values their family more than anything else, for example, they'll get out of bed and show up at work even if it's cold and raining outside, because they want to provide for their family. However, if someone values their own personal comfort more than anything else, they'll stay in bed if they see that it looks too cold and wet outside.

Values impacts what we do. Values also shape the way we address people, how we work, how we listen, and how we evaluate information. They differentiate what is important and what isn't to us.

In my company, we value service above everything else and you'll hear that in how we communicate to our employees and our customers.

Beliefs

Beliefs are the presumption that we have about the world and things around us.

During communication it is important to know someone's beliefs, as many of the views that come up during a conversation are based on certain sets of beliefs and preconceived notions. When discussing controversial topics, it's important to be careful about infringing on a person's belief system.

Beliefs are built up over many years through the experiences that we live through. An employee that joins your team from another company, for example, will have a set of beliefs about how to work with others and how to communicate with customers. That's why you'll always hear me talk about the importance of hiring superstars – because, in my experience, their beliefs will be more closely aligned with the success of your company than any other employee you might hire.

Beliefs are built on our experiences and they are foundational for us to understand the world. However, beliefs can change. So if you have beliefs that are impacting your communication, consider how you can change them to communicate more effectively.

Memories

This filter is all about our recollection of past events. Memory plays a very important role in human communication. It helps to maintain the thread of a conversation. Moreover, past experiences help us react and give feedback, whether negative or positive, to topics during a conversation.

That's why it's so important to maintain consistency in your workplace. If you joke around with your employees excessively, you embed that set of memories in your employees and they'll come to expect it. Then, if you have to remove someone from your company, you face an uphill communication battle because they remember you as a joking friend rather than as their leader.

Or consider the case of a customer who had a bad experience when hiring a previous home service company. Even though it wasn't your company, they may remember all the nice things that other company said before ripping them off… and that memory will influence how they interpret your communication.

People will combine memories from all different areas of their lives – both contemporary memories and ones from their childhood – to help them listen.

Although you won't always know what memories are influencing a listener, your awareness that they are being influenced by those memories can inform you as you communicate with them, and it can remind you to choose your words carefully and to watch for how your communication is accepted.

Decisions

This is the final filter, and it is linked to memories. If we have made some good, bad or indifferent decisions in the past, we have created some empowering or disempowering beliefs, either about the decision itself or about the outcome.

Those decisions will shape how we speak and how we understand. For example, your customer has already made a decision about your company before your expert even shows up at the door.

That's the reason that I spend so long talking about the Framework For Service in my book *The Secrets Of Business Mastery*. The Framework For Service lays out the step-by-step process that all customers go through from the moment they first contact us, all the way through to the moment when they receive a call from our automated survey after the service is completed. It's designed to help shape the decisions of customers because we want them to feel served by our company even before the expert arrives at their door.

Take Action!

___ Stop doing actions (Actions you currently do now but should stop doing)

_____

_____

___ Keep doing actions (Actions you currently do now and should keep doing)

_____

_____

___ Start doing actions (Actions you don't do now but should start doing)

_____

_____

__ Who will do new actions? (Assign the action to yourself or someone else)

_____

_____

__ By when? (When will these actions be complete?)

_____

_____

LASER-FOCUSED TACTIC #4: LEADING BY COMMUNICATION

If you need a reason to study communication, here it is: You are a leader, which means you have a team who you expect to complete their work according to the standards and expectations to you set. You communicate those standards and expectations to your team, you communicate instruction, training, and correction to them, and most importantly you build rapport with your team and discover why they want to work with you so you can inspire them to give their very best at all times.

One of the strategies to become a better leader is to become a better communicator. (There are other strategies to become a better leader, of course, and I discuss many of them in my book *Secrets Of Leadership Mastery* and in my podcast Secrets Of Business Mastery – you'll find that many of the lessons in the book you're reading right now expand on the lessons in *Secrets Of Leadership Mastery* and in my podcast).

How do you lead by communication?

It starts with using the communication skills you learn in this book to build rapport with your team, even before they ever come to work with you. As you build rapport, you'll understand them better and they'll understand you better; you'll build a trust on which you can serve each other as employer/employee. And, you'll also discover their "why" – the reason that they come to work in the first place. Knowing their why helps you as you communicate with them on an ongoing basis because you can bring back the importance of the why in their life. For example, an employee who is feeling discouraged might be encouraged by you when you remind them that they are working to put their children through college. That's information you elicit from communication.

Communication also enables you to train your team. You communicate your expectations, standards, and minimum levels and you explain how you want your employees to act and work and represent your company. And communication works in the other direction here, too: As I explain in my book *The Secrets Of Business Mastery*, as you train someone in a new skill, get them to "train" it back to you. Once they can teach it, they know it. Therefore, you are using your employee's skill of communication to reinforce what you train them and to show you whether or not your training has been effective.

Communication will also inspire your team. Don't just think of communication as a tool that you can use to get your point across – think of it as a way to raise your entire business to the next level. As I say frequently, don't just manage… lead! Leaders use communication to inspire their team and encourage them to press forward. The history books are full of military leaders who gathered armies (often unprepared and ill-equipped armies of young men who would rather be farming), and the leader use the only tool they had – their words – to inspire those unqualified warriors to perform great feats on the battlefield. That is the power of inspiration and you can do the same thing in your business.

You can also use communication to give and receive feedback – such as feedback you might give to an employee as part of their performance review. I devote an entire chapter to this later in this book.

Leaders communicate – they use it to connect with their team, they use it to train their team, they use it to inspire their team, and they use it to give and receive feedback. Of course you'll use communication in other ways in your business but if you master these four components of leadership communication, you'll have mastered the most common components of communication in your business.

Communication At Different Levels In Leadership

Not all leaders will communicate in the same way all the time. As your company grows, there will be additional layers of leadership and each of those layers will have to communicate in different ways.

For example, if you have several dozen employees and a few layers of leadership, you might have a team leader who communicates to his team about what they're doing that day, and who communicates to his leaders about what how things are going. And, you might have another layer of leadership who communicates with team leaders about what needs to be accomplished, and who communicates to the higher level leadership about how things are going. And, you might have the highest level of leadership (sometimes called "upper management" or "the executive level") who communicates with the company.

Of course it's different for every company but my point is: every layer of leadership will have different goals and requirements for communication; their scope of communication is different. At the team level, team leaders are talking about practical actions that need to be taken today on a specific job, while at the upper level, executive leaders are talking about concepts and strategies that need to be taken over the next quarter or year. Both teams are working toward specific targets but those targets are very different, therefore the communication that the leadership at each level has is very different.

Take Action!

___ Stop doing actions (Actions you currently do now but should stop doing)

_____

_____

___ Keep doing actions (Actions you currently do now and should keep doing)

_____

_____

___ Start doing actions (Actions you don't do now but should start doing)

_____

_____

___ Who will do new actions? (Assign the action to yourself or someone else)

_____

_____

___ By when? (When will these actions be complete?)

_____

_____

LASER-FOCUSED TACTIC #5: YOUR BRAIN HAS A DELETE BUTTON (AND IT'S HURTING YOU)

Communication is the complex process where you take your idea and try to replicate it in your listener's mind using words and non-verbal components. But there are several other factors that will influence whether that message is understood correctly.

And there's another challenge: Once the idea is in your listener's mind, it needs to stay there... but it often doesn't. There is often a distortion of information due to deletion.

Although we might like to think that we hear and understand everything told to us, or that our listeners hear and understand everything we say, the truth is we only pay attention to certain aspects of the information. This can lead to misunderstanding... and unwanted outcomes.

It's not that the ideas themselves are actually removed from our brain – they just get mixed up with other ideas or forgotten. That's why we make shopping lists! There are so many thoughts and facts in our mind, all competing for the same space, it's easy to see why some information gets distorted or seemingly deleted.

So how can you ensure that your listener remembers what you communicate? Here are some strategies to help. These won't always be applicable in every situation but you may find a combination of them will work for you.

1. Create a structure or framework. When you have something that you want your team to do over and over, communicate it within the context of a structure. That's why I use the Framework For Service that I talk about in my book *The Secrets Of Business Mastery*. The Framework For Service lists out a customer interaction step-by-step. When I communicate information to them about serving a customer, it makes more sense to communicate it in the context of the framework, and it becomes easier for them to remember as a daily practice.

2. Use vivid language and stories. People are hardwired to remember stories more than most other types of communication. Perhaps it's because we find stories informative and entertaining at the same time, and perhaps it's because we encounter stories as a communication method right from childhood. Using engaging and vivid language, as well as stories, will help you to implant the information in your listener's mind. Try it: Give one person 5 facts to remember and list them as a list of 5 things. Then give another person the same 5 facts but weave them into a story. Ask them each to tell you a day later what those 5 facts are the person you told the story to will almost always remember more than the person who received just the facts. Stories are also a great tool to help customers understand a complex situation that might be too technical otherwise. Even I used a type of story in an earlier chapter when I talked about the communication process being like a machine or an assembly line.

3. Use rhyming, alliteration, or acronyms, or other verbal tools. Another way to help get people to remember is to use verbal tools like rhyming, alliteration, and acronyms. Although this sounds childish and simplistic, it works and we rely on it every day.

- **Rhyming**: When you were first learning to use a screwdriver, did someone ever tell you "righty tighty lefty loosy" or something similar? Sure, you don't need that now but it was helpful at the time. You might have an appropriate rhyme in your workplace that helps you to remember something.

- **Alliteration**: This is when all words in a list start with the same letter. For example, you might encourage your team to make sure the customer **S**miles, is **S**atisfied, and **S**ays they'll refer their friends or family to you. You might call this the "3 S" program and it's an easy-to-remember checklist that your team can go through when they are at someone's home.

- **Acronyms**: This is when the first letters of a phrase or list of words can be spelled out. Harder to remember acronyms don't really spell anything but easier to remember acronyms spell out another word. For example, when your expert shows up at a customer's door, perhaps you want them to **G**reet the customer, **I**ntroduce themselves, **T**hank the customer for calling, and **A**sk if where they parked is okay. Internally, you might call this your "GITA" greeting, and it's an instant way to help your employees remember what to do whenever they show up at a customer's home.

There are other verbal tools besides these but these three are the most commonly used to help you embed your ideas in your listener's minds.

4. Ask the person to repeat the information back to you. In some cases, especially when giving specific step-by-step instructions, it's important to know that the person understood what you are saying. One way to gauge someone else's understanding (and your ability to communicate!) is to have them repeat the information back to you. Do they repeat it back word-for-word as you said it? That's okay, although it only shows that they memorized what you said. It's even better if they repeat it back accurately but in their own words (which shows that they understood what you wanted and interpreted it for themselves). If someone repeats back the information but misses something, that's a gap you can reinforce.

5. Teach the information to you: When you ask someone to repeat the information back to you, it's a helpful indicator to see if they understood what you said. And in some cases that might be all you need. For example, if you're asking them to order something for you from a supplier, then repeating back the information is enough.

But sometimes, especially when there's a new skill involved, you want to make sure that the person really understands what you have communicated to them. So ask them to teach it to you. Of course you already know it but when they speak to you as if they were teaching it to you for the first time, you get a sense of just how well they understood the skill you showed them. Teaching back to you is the most powerful tool for memory and reinforcement.

Everyone's brain has a delete key. We don't mean to delete the things we hear but sometimes it happens. These tools will help you to keep it from happening and ensure that information is retained.

Take Action!

___ Stop doing actions (Actions you currently do now but should stop doing)

_____

_____

__ Keep doing actions (Actions you currently do now and should keep doing)

_____

_____

__ Start doing actions (Actions you don't do now but should start doing)

_____

_____

__ Who will do new actions? (Assign the action to yourself or someone else)

_____

_____

__ By when? (When will these actions be complete?)

_____

_____

LASER-FOCUSED TACTIC #6: HOW TO SEE THROUGH SOMEONE ELSE'S EYES

In a previous chapter, I mentioned about how meta programs influence how people communicate. Meta programs are a set of thought and behavior patterns that operate beyond the conscious level. Meta programs are like the DNA of your communication and they control your attention during conversation, habitual linguistic patterns, and body language.

In this chapter, I want to explore meta programs in greater detail so you understand what they are and how the work.

Meta programs go a long way in predicting someone's actions as well as how they will understand your communication. When I sit down to write my magazine Home ServiceMAX, I keep these in mind because every article will be interpreted slightly differently by readers, depending on their meta programs.

There are no right or wrong meta programs. There are several meta programs, but let's take a look at the top six that are used in everyday business:

- Towards/Away from
- Frame of Reference
- Sameness/Difference
- Reason
- Chunk Size
- Convincer

Towards/Away From

"Towards" people always strive to achieve an outcome. They want to move towards something. In making moves towards a certain outcome or goal, Towards people find it difficult to recognize what they need to avoid. Instead they concentrate and focus on what they will get when the outcome is achieved.

On the other hand, "Away from" people make a concerted effort to avoid a certain situation. They don't want to experience loss or discomfort and want to move away from something.

What do you do if you want to know what type of person one of your workers is? Ask these types of questions:

- What do you want?
- What will having "xyz" give you?
- What do you want in "xyz"?

This is what his response will tell you:

- Toward people will tell you what they want.
- Away from people will tell you what they don't want.

Once you've determined which type of person you're dealing with, you can determine the best way to communicate with him.

This is what you do when in negotiations with people:

- Towards: Work out what their goals are, and what you can do to help them achieve these goals. Focus on the outcome, and what it will give them.
- Away from: Work out what you can do to help them avoid what they don't want. Work out and anticipate potential problems, and assure them that these can be minimized or avoided.

You can manage such people in this fashion:

- Towards: Offer incentives, i.e. an outcome. Emphasize their goals, and what and how they can achieve them.
- Away from: Use sanctions. Be aware that these people are usually the ones to bring up problems.

Influencing Language
Towards: Get, achieve, attain, include, obtain, have, want, etc.
Away from: Not have, avoid, don't want, keep away from, get rid of, etc.

Frame Of Reference
The second major meta program is frame of reference.
This is all about how people evaluate things, and can be split into two types, Internal people and External people.

Internal People stand true to their opinion, and evaluate based on what they think is appropriate. They make all decisions themselves, and can have difficulty accepting other people's feedback and direction.

External People evaluate based on what other people think is appropriate. They need others to guide, direct and motivate them. Since they cannot decide for themselves, they need external references.

How do you know if a team member is an Internal or an External person?

Ask this type of question: "How do you know that you have done a good job?"

The response will speak for itself.

- Internal people will tell you that they decide when they've done a good job.
- External people tell you that they know because other people or outside information sources tell them.

When you are negotiating with these people, this is what you should do:

- Internal: Emphasize to the person that inside they will know it is right. Say that the choice is theirs. Don't bother with external factors or what other people think - they will not be interested in this.
- External: Emphasize what others think. Give data and information to back up your points. Give feedback and reassurance.

Manage the different types in this way:

- Internal: They have difficulty in accepting feedback or praise. They like to decide for themselves, and don't like to be told what to do. They do best when they have little or no supervision. Let them be, as much as you can. Don't try to force your opinion down their throat.
- External: These people need close management. They need constant feedback and re-assurance about how well they are doing. They need to be told what to do, how to do it and how well they are doing it. Be supportive and encouraging to them.

Influencing language:

- Internal: You know best, you'll know when it's right, only you can decide, it's up to you, etc.
- External: Can I give you some feedback, I will let you know, the facts show, other people think that, etc.

Sameness/Difference

This meta program is about people's perceptions of likeness and differences.

There are four main categories:

- 'Sameness' people will notice things that are the same, or match their previous experiences. They dislike change.
- 'Sameness with exception' people will first notice similarities, and will then notice the differences. They prefer slow or gradual change.
- 'Difference with exception' people will notice differences, and then similarities. They like change and variety.
- 'Difference' people will notice things that are different. They love change and want it all of the time.

So, how do you know what type of person someone is?

Ask these types of questions: "What is the relationship between these three objects? What is the relationship between this X and a previous Y?"

What their response will tell you:

- Sameness people will tell you what similar qualities the objects have.
- Sameness with exception people will tell you first how things are similar, and then tell you what differences they have.
- Difference with exception people will tell you first how things are different, and then give you the similarities.
- Difference people will plainly tell you what the differences are.

In negotiations with these people:

- Sameness: Stress areas of agreement. Do not discuss differences. Discuss areas of similarities and explain how you both want the same thing.
- Sameness with exception: First stress similarities, and then point out the differences. Talk about change as a gradual slow process.
- Difference with exception: First stress how things are different, and then talk about similarities. Focus on change and new solutions.
- Difference: Stress how things are different. Do not mention similarities. Talk in terms of massive change and revolutionary.

34

In managing these people:

- Sameness: Have them do things the same way. They hate variety, so don't talk about it. Instead, talk about continuity.
- Sameness with exception: Have them do the same things, but with gradual improvements and changes. Initiate a gradual process of change by talking about it.
- Difference with exception: Downplay commonality by emphasizing improvements and changes. Stress different ways to do the job, and make changes frequently.
- Difference: Talk about the differences. These people will get bored at repetitive tasks. So have them do something new all the time.

Influencing language

Sameness: Same, same as, maintain, keep doing, in common, keep the same, usual, similar, etc.

Sameness with exception: Better, more, less, gradual, although, but, same except, etc.

Difference with exception: Different, new, changed, change, unusual, etc.

Difference: Different, new, radical, unique, revolutionary, etc.

Reason

The meta program regarding reason is all about people's opinions towards making choices, developing options and following procedures.

Here, there are two types of people: Options and Procedures.

- Options people are very good at developing choices. They want to experiment, and therefore tend to be rule breakers or benders rather than rule followers. They are very good at making improvements and developing new procedures or alternatives to old ones.
- Procedures people are good at following procedures, and thus, are rule followers. But they do not know how to generate them. When they do not have a procedure to follow, they get stuck.

How do you know what type a particular person is?

Ask this type of question: Why did you choose 'xyz'? The response will tell you:

- Options people will give you the reasons why they did it.

- Procedures people will tell you a story about how they came to do
  what they did. They don't talk about choices or options. They give
  you the impression that they don't have choices.

In negotiations with these people:
- Options people: Do not follow a fixed procedure for the
  negotiation. Concentrate on the choices and possibilities, and
  discuss all of them.
- Procedures people: Lay out a procedure for the negotiation.
  Don't give options or choices, and don't expect them to decide
  on alternatives.

In managing these people:

- Options people: Talk about the possibilities and alternatives.
  Tell them to think of new ways. Do not expect them to follow
  routines. Make sure they do not violate procedures.
- Procedures people: Stress the procedures to do the work. Make
  sure there are procedures in place, and that the person
  understands them. Be prepared to assist if the procedure fails.

Influencing Language
- Options people: Alternatives, reasons, options, choices,
  possibilities etc.
- Procedures people: Correct way, procedure, known way, right
  way, proven way etc.

Chunk Size

The need for details in an individual's life throws two categories of
people here: the detailed/specific person, and, those who prefer large
chunks of information or the global person.
- Specific people like to work with all the small details. They like
  to understand and go into pieces of work with the minutest of
  detail.
- Global people like to talk in big picture, and are not interested
  in details at all. They are conceptual and abstract. They'd rather
  give you the overall framework or brief of what is happening,
  than go into details.

You know when someone is specific and when someone is global just by asking any question and analyzing the response.

- Specific people will give you all the details, and go to great lengths to explain everything when you ask questions. Specific people become frustrated with global people because there is no detail in what they say.
- Global people give you an overview without details. They tend to use large generalizations. Global people become frustrated with specific people because they go too far into detail.

If you are a specific person in your management style, and your team members are global people, it could create some tension in communicating with them. You'll need to learn to speak to your technicians and other employees no matter what their style is.

In negotiations with these people:

- Specific people: Avoid generalizations and vagueness. Break things down into detail and be specific. Present things in logical sequences.
- Global people: Avoid details and present the bigger picture.

In managing these people:

- Specific people: Tell the person in detail what needs to be done and ensure that there is a logical sequence. Do not expect him to think about the bigger picture.
- Global people: Skip the details and give the person a broad overview. Tell them what the end game is, and let them fill in the rest.

Influencing language:

- Specific people: Next, then, precisely, exactly, specifically, first, second, details etc.
- Global people: Big picture, framework, in brief, result, generally, overview etc.

Convincer

People make decisions and are convinced for only one of four reasons:

- It looks right
- It feels right
- It sounds right
- It makes sense

How do you find out what kind of people use each reason to make a decision on a service call?

Ask them this question: "Why did you decide xyz?"

What their response will tell you:

- Looks right people do things because the representation that they make to themselves is a picture that literally looks right. They will use visual words when describing their decision. For instance, they may say that they took certain steps to fix a leak because they saw the water coming from a pipe.

- Feels right people do things because the representation they make to themselves is a sensation in some part of their body which literally feels right. They use kinesthetic words when describing their decision.

- Sounds right people do things because the representation they make to themselves is a series of words which literally sounds right to them. They will use auditory words when describing their decision. They may make a decision on how to resolve a problem at a service call based on what the homeowner tells them.

- Makes sense people do things because the representation they make to themselves is based on logic, which in their own mind, they know, is correct. They will use auditory words when describing their decision, and they will use facts, data and reason. These people are often very comfortable with their knowledge about a subject, and will go with what their training tells them.

In negotiations with these people, use the appropriate language patterns that match their decision process. If you are providing learning materials, make sure they are appropriate for the person – i.e. pictures, diagrams, facts, data etc.

In managing these people:

- Looks right people: Paint a picture in words, draw a diagram, and give them pictorial references to explain things to them. Let their imagination flow free. Show them how to do it.

- Feels right people: Get their internal senses working, by letting them discern what they need to do. Let them get their hands on the task, and touch, feel and experience what needs to be done.

- Sounds right people: Have them describe to themselves in internal dialogue, or in an appropriate tone of voice, what they are supposed to do. Tell them things. Tell them what others say.

38

They will make decisions after exploring all that they have heard.

- Makes sense people: They are the logical ones, so give reasons for what you want them to do. Let them read instructions on how to do the job. Give them facts, statistics and data.

Influencing language:

Use appropriate language based on what suits each type of person, to help them make their decisions.

Take Action!

__ Stop doing actions (Actions you currently do now but should stop doing)

_____

_____

__ Keep doing actions (Actions you currently do now and should keep doing)

_____

_____

__ Start doing actions (Actions you don't do now but should start doing)

_____

_____

__ Who will do new actions? (Assign the action to yourself or someone else)

_____

_____

___ By when? (When will these actions be complete?)

_____

_____

LASER-FOCUSED TACTIC #7: ELICITING THINKING PATTERNS THROUGH EYE MOVEMENT

In the late 1970s and early 1980s, researchers discovered that people move their eyes a certain way when they think.

They also noticed that students, when asked a series of questions, had structured pattern eye movements while thinking. Researchers concluded that by looking at someone's eyes, you could tell how they think.

You can tell the way people are constructing their thoughts by observing their eye movements. The basic rule of eye movement pattern works this way:

Eye Direction	Meaning
Looking up	Visualizing
Looking horizontally left or right	Remembering/constructing sounds
Looking down to the left	Accessing feelings
Looking down to the right	Talking to self

You might be wondering why this matters. The simple answer is: you can watch people's eye movements and get a clue about how they are constructing their answers when they talk to you. When you ask an employee to describe conversation with a customer, they might be look down and to the left and that indicates that the conversation had some emotional connection – perhaps it was stressful.

Or if you're talking to a customer and you ask them to describe the sound that their air conditioning unit was making, they might look left or right to remember the sound.

The point of this knowledge is to provide you with another clue about how someone is processing information.

In general, people tend to process information in five different ways – visual recall, visual construct, auditory recall, auditory construct, and kinesthetic. (Often, people prefer one over the others). I've listed the five ways below to help you see how this information can be useful when you're talking to customers and to employees.

41

Visual Recall

This is when you recall images from the past. You are drawing them from your memory, and these are things you have seen before.

Type of questions to ask to aid a worker's visual recall:

- "What do our service trucks look like?"
- "What did you see when you looked at the homeowner's sink?"
- "What tools did you use to fix that electrical wiring issue?"

Visual Construct

This happens when you try to picture something you have never seen before. These are images you are making up in your head, or basing on knowledge you have acquired.

Type of questions to ask to aid someone's visual construct:

- "What would a blown fuse look like?"
- "What would you see if you knew a heating and air conditioning unit needed to be replaced?"

Auditory Recall

This is when you remember sounds or voices that you have heard before, or things that you have previously said to yourself. These sounds are stored in your memory bank and you are actually extracting it from its location. It's this ability that helps you recognize a voice over the phone even before the person says his/her name. Type of questions to ask to aid someone's auditory recall:

- "Can you remember how that woman sounded when her wedding ring went down the drain?"
- "What was the last thing I said?"

Auditory Construct

This is when you are making up sounds that you have never heard before. The type of questions to ask to aid someone's auditory construct:

- "What would a toilet sound like if it had a loose connection?"

Kinesthetic

This involves accessing your feelings or emotions about something. Types of questions to ask to access someone's feelings.

- "What does it feel like to touch a dirty air filter?"
- "What does it feel like to know how to repair a blown circuit breaker?"

Since communication is all about rapport building, we have to be able to mirror and match another person's preferred learning and thinking style in order to communicate in the most effective way.

By observing words that people use, and how they move their eyes, we can understand their strategy. However, don't always look for strategies in people's eyes, because not all eye movements indicate one.

In order to communicate effectively we need to study action signals put forward by people, and then modify our behavior, physiology and words so that they can easily relate to us.

Take Action!

___ Stop doing actions (Actions you currently do now but should stop doing)

_____

_____

___ Keep doing actions (Actions you currently do now and should keep doing)

_____

_____

___ Start doing actions (Actions you don't do now but should start doing)

_____

_____

__ Who will do new actions? (Assign the action to yourself or someone else)

_____

_____

__ By when? (When will these actions be complete?)

_____

_____

LASER-FOCUSED TACTIC #8: HOW TO CONNECT WITH PEOPLE EFFORTLESSLY

You meet different types of people every day. It is not possible to make and maintain a good relationship with all of them, because you don't connect with every single one of them. However, it's important for you to create positive interactions with them – especially in dealing with employees or customers.

Communication needs to be results-oriented. Building rapport is the ultimate tool for producing results, and is vital for effective communication. As the foundation for any meaningful interaction, rapport makes you more memorable and can be critical for your business.

Building rapport is similar to building a bridge over a river. The stronger the bridge, the more it can carry. In a relationship, you can ask for more if you have better rapport with the other person. Good rapport will help your technicians and other team members stay motivated toward company goals, and when you build such relationships with customers, they will show loyalty to your company when they need services.

Communication is much more than an exchange of words. In fact, 93 percent of all communication comes down to the tonality of your voice and your body language – your words make up just a small fraction of the total "process" of communication. Building rapport is far more than just talking about common experiences.

Some people easily build rapport with others. Even if you are a master rapport builder, you've also had times when you thought, "Oh, what am I going to do and say next?"

Everyone has these experiences. Maybe you've had an experience where you were tired and had a terrible headache, and a friend or colleague came in, full of energy, wanting to talk your head off. Perhaps the situation has been reversed, and you have turned out to be the irritating friend. You can likely relate to either of these situations – but by building rapport, you can overcome most of them. Let's now take a look at the six things you need to do to build rapport:

1. Match The Person's Sensory Modality
People like to have relationships with those who think and behave like themselves, or even with those who have similar backgrounds. Matching

45

and mirroring the way others think and talk is a good way to build rapport with them.

There is slight difference between mirroring and matching. Mirroring is quite similar to looking into a mirror. The time difference between the actions of both parties is negligible. However, with matching you have to wait for your turn to repeat the action of the other party.

2. Mirror The Person's Physiology

Have you ever noticed that a group of teenagers who are friends bear similarities in their clothing, vocabulary and movements? Maybe you and your spouse have similar mannerisms and facial expressions after years of marriage. People who are in rapport have a tendency to dress in a similar way or have matching body language.

Mirroring the physiology of someone you're talking to can make them feel comfortable. Copying the person's posture, facial expressions, hand gestures, movements and even eye blinking, will cause their body to say unconsciously to the mind that "this person is like myself!" This is a great rapport-building technique with customers, since it helps them trust you.

3. Match The Person's Voice

You should match the tone, tempo, timbre and the volume of the person's voice. If the person is slow and deliberate, he will feel comfortable if you are the same way. You should also try, when you speak, to use the keywords that they use.

4. Match The Person's Breathing

If there is a big difference in the breathing pattern of two people in conversation, both of them would feel uncomfortable. If you want to build rapport with someone, you need to match the rhythm of breathing of the other person by moving your foot or finger at the same pace.

5. Match How The Person Deals With Information

People deal with information differently. Some are detail-oriented, and some prefer to keep it brief. You need to match the other person's way of dealing with information. If you are talking to a customer who wants to know every detail of a repair or installation, broken down by cost, be prepared to share that. In other circumstances, you may meet someone who just wants to know the overview of what they are paying you to do at their house.

If you get this wrong you will find it very difficult to build rapport, as the detail-oriented person will be yearning for more information, and the big picture type will soon be yawning.

6. Match Common Experiences

Suppose you are a long way from home and met someone who is a total stranger, and discovered they are from your own hometown. Before long, you will find yourself in a very lively conversation with them, looking for experiences in common.

Finding commonality is crucial to building relationships. If both parties have matching experiences, interests, backgrounds, values and beliefs, they have greater chance of a rapport. For instance, customers will appreciate knowing about your local ties, especially if you have a large service area.

One point to bear in mind is that you need to be subtle when you are matching and mirroring. Be careful not to step over any boundaries and make someone uncomfortable, or to come across as if you are mocking the other person. Typically, the other person will not notice it.

You can develop your ability to observe other people that you will begin to see and even predict people's reactions to communications. This is known as calibration, and is a way of determining whether you are in rapport with someone.

Take Action!

___ Stop doing actions (Actions you currently do now but should stop doing)

_____

_____

__ Keep doing actions (Actions you currently do now and should keep doing)

_____

_____

__ Start doing actions (Actions you don't do now but should start doing)

_____

_____

__ Who will do new actions? (Assign the action to yourself or someone else)

_____

_____

__ By when? (When will these actions be complete?)

_____

_____

LASER-FOCUSED TACTIC #9: HOW TO MAKE SMALL TALK WITH PEOPLE

The ability to enter a new or unfamiliar situation and begin to engage others in conversation is a widely admired skill. Many people assume it is an innate ability. Actually, the ability to make small talk is not a natural gift, but an acquired skill.

This sought-after skill can be learned and perfected through practice. This skill can play a vital role in boosting your self-confidence and can be critical in your professional life.

For most people, starting a conversation with unfamiliar people is a difficult and painful task. But when you are running a service business, it is vital that you, and your employees, are able to converse with customers and others you may deal with in the course of your daily business. While dealing with repairs and installations at their home, you are likely to have the opportunity to talk to homeowners about other things.

This session is all about how to communicate with people you have never met before. You can use the techniques even with people whom you find really incommunicative or in a difficult situation.

Meeting people for the first time can be a very daunting task – especially if you're going to their home to fulfill a need. However, if you understand other people and how they like to communicate, and what they like to talk about, then meeting people for the first time can be an enjoyable experience.

The main difficulty you face in starting small talk with an unfamiliar person is that you put yourself under tremendous pressure to talk. You will start asking yourself questions like:

- What should I talk about?
- What should I say?
- How will I fill the silence in the conversation?

You are very concerned about how others are evaluating you while you are making small talk. You are concerned not only for the evaluation during the talk, but also for the judgment that goes beyond the conversation. You are too busy thinking of what to say that you forget about communicating with the other person!

Become An Expert Listener

The best conversationalists in the world are the best listeners. You must resist the urge to dominate the conversation. In fact, the person who says the least is often the best communicator. Then why should you be racking your brains thinking of things to say every time?

In a conversation, if you are listening, it means the other person is talking. Becoming an expert listener makes you a good conversationalist. During the conversation, lean slightly forward, face the other person directly, and don't miss a single word. Most people are poor listeners because they are busy preparing a reply while the other person is still speaking.

When you go into a situation where you are meeting someone for the first time, you need to be very much focused on him. You must treat that person as if he is the most important person in the world. Ask questions that evoke interest in him and be intrigued about his answers. Practicing listening in casual conversations you have will also help you learn how to listen when customers are describing a problem or need.

Small talk depends very much on your ability to ask questions and to listen attentively to the answers. Wait for your turn to speak. The other person may ask about you at any point during the conversation. When that happens, don't talk for too long. Always try to ask open-ended questions.

So, how can you start and hold a good conversation, and learn how to make small talk that leads to you helping a person with their needs?

To do this, it is important to understand what other people like to talk about. Here are the top five most common topics, in order:

1. Themselves. Do you love to share great stories about how you achieved your greatest accomplishments, or how you met your spouse, or about the best trip you ever took? You're not alone.

Yes, people love to talk about themselves.

The best way to build rapport with someone and to hold a conversation is to allow them to talk about their favorite subject.

Always ask for a person's opinion, their stand, and more importantly, about their achievements.

If you're at a customer's house and you notice a picture of them in an interesting or exotic place, ask them about it. "Oh, I see you visited the Great Wall of China. Tell me about it!"

Ask questions to get them to talk about themselves, and then ask some more questions, and then some more. You'll find that people revel in the opportunity.

2. Their Own Opinions. Everyone has an opinion about something. And people love to air their opinions on anything and everything. You can ask a variety of questions that will elicit a strong response based on a person's opinion, such as:

- "What do you think of the way New England has played this year?"
- "What is your opinion on the tax reform bill?"
- "What do you think of XYZ program?"

Ask these questions - you will have them talking for hours. Be careful of a couple of things: First, be careful to ask appropriate opinions at appropriate times (for example, it's not be appropriate to ask a customer for their opinion on politics or religion). Second, be careful not to be argumentative if your opinion differs.

3. Other People. Who doesn't want to gossip? People love to talk about other people. You can easily start a conversation by talking about someone the other party has an interest in. For instance, here's a conversation starter: "I heard your niece is the new Ms. California. Is she planning for a career in modeling?" You will get everything from how much the niece loves the person to her appointments for the next ten years.

Although this kind of conversation might occasionally be appropriate in a social situation, it is rarely appropriate in a professional setting, between employees or between employees and customers. I have simply included it in this list because it is one of the top five topics people love to talk about. You will need to judge the appropriateness of this topic in the situation you're in and you may need to gracefully change the topic if the conversation lingers on someone who is not present.

4. Things. A question such as, "I love your car, what model is it?" will get a quick, enthusiastic response from most people. Everyone is proud of their possessions and will never miss a chance to talk about them. You will surely get a detailed description of the vehicle for the above question.

5. You. So you have reached the bottom of the list. Unfortunately, the last thing people want to talk about is you.

As you are trying to keep the conversation focused on the other person, you will have to wait for your turn to speak about yourself. And worse, you cannot talk about what you want to. Whatever you say should be connected to what the other person has already said.

Making The First Move

Another reason people avoid small talk is because they develop social anxiety around whether they might be rejected or judged.

While this might be an acute feeling in a social situation, there is no reason to feel this way in your business: you are the leader, your team is made up of peers who respect you, and your customers are eager for your ideas – so it's very different than a social situation and people are looking to you with respect, not judgment.

Take a deep breath, go to the person and ask an opening question.

Small talk is the foundation of any serious conversation. So it's always good to start off with small talk. Start with simple topics of conversation and then move on to the real reason for your interaction.

Take Action!

___ Stop doing actions (Actions you currently do now but should stop doing)

_____

_____

___ Keep doing actions (Actions you currently do now and should keep doing)

_____

_____

___ Start doing actions (Actions you don't do now but should start doing)

_____

_____

___ Who will do new actions? (Assign the action to yourself or someone else)

_____

_____

___ By when? (When will these actions be complete?)

_____

_____

LASER-FOCUSED TACTIC #10: GIVING AND RECEIVING FEEDBACK

Feedback is a powerful communication tool. It can help people understand their own behavior, and find out things about themselves that they might not have considered or realized. The ability to give and solicit feedback makes you a good communicator.

Giving feedback is one of the most difficult things in communication… and, in fact, in all of leadership and business ownership! Some people struggle with providing proper feedback in their personal and professional lives. Without knowing how to give feedback, it can be uncomfortable and unpleasant for both the giver and the receiver.

Feedback should be given in a way that the receiver can use it to either make improvements or keep up the good work. This communication tool is widely used in education, and is essential for learning and continuous improvement. Constructive criticism and feedback motivates people.

So before we go any further, change your thinking about feedback: stop thinking of it as a negative thing you have to do as a leader and instead start thinking about it as a powerful tool to serve everyone more effectively. When your feedback comes from that attitude, your employees will appreciate and even seek out your feedback because they know that you are helping them become more aligned in your business.

Giving feedback is an integral part of the coaching process that provides your staff members with support and direction, and ultimately results in increased participation. Both positive feedback (praise) and negative feedback (constructive criticism) have a part to play. It is the best way to convey your staff what you think about a particular work or performance. Proper feedback will help your employees improve and will motivate them to continue working toward company goals.

The following are the seven principles of feedback:

1. Choose correct timing for feedback. Feedback is most helpful and effective when given at the earliest opportunity after the given behavior or incident has occurred. Immediate feedback will help to reinforce a correct behavior, and increase the chances of it recurring.

Corrective feedback is most effective when given as soon as possible. If a wrong behavior is not corrected with corrective feedback at the earliest possible moment, the staff member may repeat it and set a bad precedent.

But, in the case of corrective feedback, the receiver's willingness to hear it is very important.

2. Ask for self-assessment. In a communication process, the willingness of the receiver to hear the feedback is very important. To ensure the participation of the other party, the sender needs to create an open atmosphere before giving corrective feedback.

Asking the person for self-assessment may help involve him in the feedback process. It can create an open atmosphere and promote dialogue between the sender and the receiver. In fact, many people may not be aware of the gravity of the mistakes they have committed or the job they have done well.

Allowing the person to voice his opinions before providing your own assessment of performance can lead to more positive results. Such opportunities for self-assessment may help the person to assume more responsibility without supervision.

3. Focus on specifics. "I liked the way you trained your subordinate. You outlined the procedure in writing, and then listened as he relayed back to you the process. Great job!"

Feedback should not be linked to the personality or character of the person. You should focus on a specific correct or incorrect behavior. Such feedback can make the person more willing and able to change. Feedback should be specific, visible and measurable in order to be effective.

For example, when providing corrective feedback:

- Do: "When you were talking to customer xyz, I noticed that you forgot to use her name."
- Don't: "You are not building rapport with the customer."
- When providing praise:
- Do: "When you spoke to customer xyz, I noticed that you used really good open and closed questioning techniques."
- Don't: "You communicated well there."

4. Limit feedback to a few important points. Feedback should address the needs of you and the other person. However, it should be limited to a few very important points.

Good coaches and communicators identify one or two critical areas and help the person address them one at a time. Examination of many aspects of behavior at one time is too hard to be effective.

Restrict your feedback to one or two important points so that you do not overwhelm the other person with too many things to consider.

5. Provide more praise than corrective feedback. Praise is usually given for exemplary work or behavior that exceeds expectations. However, positive reinforcement can also play an important role in bringing about change.

When you give corrective feedback, remember to point out correct behaviors first. This is as important as pointing out mistakes and areas that need improvement. And always try to conclude the conversation in a positive manner.

6. Give praise for expected performance. Sometimes a positive appraisal or a word of praise can work miracles. Praise is a strong motivator and nothing is more encouraging than acceptance.

People deserve to be praised for doing their job to the expected level. In fact, positive feedback is enjoyable for both the sender and the receiver. One thing you have to keep in mind is that praising anyone who meets established standards is as important as praising the exceptional performer. Tell the person exactly why you are praising him/her in clear and specific words.

Remember, praise may be what it takes to turn an average employee into an exceptional one.

7. Develop Action Plans. Effective implementation of any process needs an action plan. You need to work together with subordinates to identify the desired performance or result and how it can be achieved. Also chose a deadline for the completion of the steps.

Useful Techniques To Use When Giving Feedback:

Open-Ended Questioning. Open-ended questions do not have a preset limit. They promote continued conversation and allow the person to give more details. They are meant to draw out more information and often give more insight into the other person's feelings.

Consider the following question: "Do you like the new program?" The question can be answered with a yes or no, or with a simple statement of fact.

Ask the following question instead: "What are your concerns about this new program?"

Use words like: What? How? Who? Tell me?

Avoid closed questions when you are trying to get more information from someone.

Avoid words like: Do you? Did you? Have you?

Also be careful with the use of "Why," especially when giving feedback. The person may think that you are blaming them, or being critical, if you use it.

Reflecting Back. You can use the other person's complaints as a tool to create an open atmosphere. This is about putting what the other person has said into your own words and replicating it. This technique is known as paraphrasing.

Paraphrasing is a good way to show that you are listening and, more importantly, that you are understanding.

For example:

> **The other person**: "I always seem to get the rough end of the stick – no one listens to me at all."
> **You**: "You seem concerned that no one listens to you, and that you seem to be getting a bad deal."

Maintaining Silence

You can convey a lot of things via silence. Moreover, you can encourage the person to take his time, and give an appropriate reply. Always give the other person time to think through his reply.

Silence is not an opportunity to feel uncomfortable or lose your interest in the conversation. Be careful to maintain eye contact and demonstrate an interest.

Summarizing

The other person needs to be convinced that you have heard everything correctly, and understood from their perspective. Summarize the output of the meeting and action plan and recite it to them. Then you can conclude the discussion and focus on planning for the future.

Example: "The three major issues you raised were…" or "To summarize then…"

Being Sensitive

A good communicator is an empathetic person. Being sensitive to the needs of the person is important as they may reject the feedback initially. Give the person space and time to think. This may help them to absorb the feedback in its intended sense.

Initiating Action and Offering Ideas

Feedback is always associated with improvement. So giving a well-structured action plan and some ideas for the betterment of the performance can be very constructive.

Consider the following example: "Can you think of an action that would help build on your skills in this area?"

Do not allow your personal opinion to reflect in the ideas you offer. You have many other opportunities to do that.

Gaining Ownership

You need to make the person feel comfortable to act in line with your feedback. For this, you can help him to integrate the feedback into his experience. Then he can have a point of view other than yours.

Linking the feedback, as much as possible, to business results and objectives will help increase ownership. Remember, any change in behavior will only occur through acceptance and ownership of the feedback by that person.

Receiving Feedback

There are times when you face the other side of the coin too. While giving feedback, remember that at some point you will also be at the 'receiving end'. So be prepared.

Etch this onto your mind: as long as the feedback comes to you in a non-judgmental and appropriate fashion, accept it is as a valuable piece of information for learning, and for your continued development as a person.

This valuable piece of information is what we call constructive feedback, and it is critical for self-development and growth.

Here are some points to remember when you receive feedback:

- Don't shy away from constructive feedback, welcome it
- Accept feedback of any sort as what it is – information
- Evaluate the feedback before responding
- Make your own choice about what you intend to do with the information

The Feedback Emotional Rollercoaster

Here's a feedback model that you should keep in mind while giving or receiving feedback. Use the acronym DAWA to remember it:

Denial: This is typically associated with jumping the gun. Most people, while receiving feedback, tend to jump at it and immediately get defensive by arguing, denying or justifying. Try to avoid it. This just gets in the way of appreciation for the information you are being given.

Anger: So you've been told that your work is not as good as it ought to be. Here comes anger, right after denial, where you said, "It's as good as always", you get angry as the feedback stews in your mind and body. The immediate reaction is to fume!

Withdrawal: Once the anger dies down, people have time to reflect and ponder on the feedback. They might think, "Well, I have been making more mistakes than I normally do." This is when people take time out to mull over the feedback and think about what it actually means.

Acceptance: The withdrawal stage is closely followed by the final part of this model – accepting the feedback, assessing its value and the consequences of ignoring it, or using it. "I *have* been making mistakes."

Another Type Of Feedback

So far I've talked about giving and receiving job-related feedback, such as you might give to an employee or even the kind of feedback that an employee might give you about their job.

But there's another type of feedback that I need to mention and it is essential to your business (and, in fact, has a greater impact even beyond your business). I'm talking about the feedback you receive from others about how you communicate.

The master of any practice (leadership, communication, martial arts, you name it) is always looking to improve and expand. And to do this, they seek out feedback from others. If you want to improve your communication, you should seek feedback from others on how you communicate.

Therefore, you should constantly and intentionally ask people for feedback on your communication. You can do this in a number of ways:

Informally: After you've given some instructions, informally ask people to repeat back what you just told them in their own words. This is a check to make sure that they understood you but it's also a check to make sure that you're communicating effectively.

You can also pause periodically in the conversation to enquire, "is what I'm saying making sense to you?" or "do you understand what I mean?" Be wary that people might just tell you that they do understand even though they don't, but it can still be helpful to pause for these brief questions.

Informally, you can also "read" people's body language and their answers back to you. If you have a great rapport with someone but suddenly an answer comes back that is extremely brief and to the point, it's a signal to you that there could be a break communication and maybe they've misunderstood something you said. (Of course there might be other factors – you just gather the clues and then you need to hunt down the answer).

Formally: There are more formal ways to gather feedback about how you're communicating. I like to do this through surveys. You can survey your employees, your customers, and even your friends and family to ask them how you are communicating. The formality is in the intention – you are expressly seeking open-ended feedback about how you communicate.

The survey might take a structured approach where you have an automated phone survey company call your customers and employees so they can answer anonymously. And if you have an honest and open communication with your friends and family, you should invite them to simply share their thoughts with you about your communication.

You don't have to change everything based on the feedback of just one or two people but if you hear over and over that there's something about the way you communicate, it's a signal to you that you might need to make a change.

Expect feedback on some of the following factors:

- Clarity (not clear enough)
- Speed of communication (too fast, too slow)
- Directness (how straightforward you are, or whether your communication meanders with stories and digressions)
- Lack of empathy
- Optimism/realism/pessimism (perhaps too much of one or not enough of another)

Communication is not a one-way street. Feedback is an essential part of communication and you should encourage it and welcome it.

Take Action!

__ Stop doing actions (Actions you currently do now but should stop doing)

_____

_____

__ Keep doing actions (Actions you currently do now and should keep doing)

_____

_____

__ Start doing actions (Actions you don't do now but should start doing)

_____

_____

__ Who will do new actions? (Assign the action to yourself or someone else)

_____

_____

__ By when? (When will these actions be complete?)

_____

_____

LASER-FOCUSED TACTIC #11: ASK GREAT QUESTIONS

One of the most powerful ways to communicate is to ask questions. When I tell this to people, I often get curious looks because people don't often associate questions with communication (communication is often thought of as the things we say, not the things we inquire about), and people believe they already know how to ask questions since it's something we do from childhood.

But there's a difference between asking questions and learning to ask great questions. The more I spend time interviewing people on my podcast Secrets Of Business Mastery, the more I realize the value of great questions as a key part of communication. Great communicators – and great leaders – ask great questions.

- Great questions enable you to grow your business in a powerful way by serving those you work for and who work for you.
- Great questions help you to build rapport with whomever you are asking questions to, and rapport is a powerful way to elevate your communication.
- Great questions allow you to understand any situation more effectively and to identify a course of action that will help you succeed in that situation.

There are, of course, other reasons to ask good questions but these are the areas I'll cover in this book. And later in this chapter I'll also share with you some strategies to help you ask better questions.

Grow Your Business With Better Questions
It doesn't matter if it's work-related or not, better questions can help you get more out of every situation and interaction you're in.

Better questions with your employees: When you learn to ask better questions of your employees, you will discover their motivations and the reasons they show up to work. For your superstar employees, you can use this improved understanding to help you inspire them to give their very best every day because they understand that by giving their best to you, you will help them achieve whatever their personal targets are in life. For example, don't just assume that every employee wants to show up to earn a paycheck and get the weekends off. Through better questions, you might discover an employee who wants to work hard because they are putting their child through college and it's something they are very proud to do. By learning this, you can build a work schedule that will help them earn enough money to put their child through college, you'll gain their respect and admiration by asking them occasionally about how their child is doing, and you can suggest that they book their holidays at times that coincide with dropping their child off at college or attending their graduation. Imagine the payoff! Your employees will see you as someone who truly has their best interests at heart and you'll get more loyal, harder-working employees! See how well you can connect with an employee just because you asked better questions?

The reverse is true as well: asking better questions of your employees may reveal that there is not a match for your company and it may make sense for them to seek employment elsewhere. While some service business owners might try to avoid this because they don't want to lose an employee or because they don't want to create conflict by letting an employee go, you can use questions to help you. After identifying that an employee's motivations and interests are not aligned with your company, ask the employee, "do you think you'll find better alignment somewhere else?"

Better questions with your vendors: When most service business owners interact with their vendors, they often ask questions like, "how can I get this cheaper?" But when you think of your vendors in the same way that you think of your employees – as people with their own motivations who you can serve – you'll ask different questions and get different answers. For example, why not ask your vendors, "how can I serve you?" and, "who else do you work with and can I serve them?" and, "how can we make our working relationship more efficient and effective?" These changes in questions will transform your working relationship and you'll get better products and services from your vendors.

Better questions with your customers: Asking better questions works well with your customers, too. When you or your experts visit a customer's house, don't just ask them about what the problem is. Go deeper. Ask them about how the problem is impacting them. This allows you to serve them at a higher level by showing how your service not only fixes the immediate problem but improves their life. And, asking this question may also give you other opportunities to serve them as well. For example, if a customer asks you for help with their hot water tank, push beyond the basic question of "what's wrong with it?" to "how is it affecting your life?" because that question might reveal that their mineral-rich water is not only impacting their hot water tank but also their drinking water and they may also benefit from a water filter.

Don't forget that you should also ask your customers for feedback. In this case, I recommend using an automated service since I've found that people are more willing to be honest with an automated call than when they are talking to a person.

These are just some of the ways that you use great questions to uncover better answers that allow you to serve those.

Build Rapport With Better Questions

As children, our natural tendency was one of curiosity. We questions everything in order to learn. Even teenagers who seem rebellious are really just living out a type of question – they're questioning whether the values of their parents or society are the values they want to live with.

Questions guided us as children and teens but as adults, we often stop asking questions, or at least we stop asking good questions. We end up giving more answers than asking more questions. Our thoughts transition from curiosity to answers, advice, and opinions. There's nothing wrong with having these, of course, but I believe questions help us to live better lives and build better businesses.

I also believe that questions help us to enjoy better relationships. Think about when you first met your spouse or significant other. There was a getting-to-know-you period when you often thought of each and frequently asked the other person questions to learn more about them. For that brief period of time, we rekindled that curiosity we had as children in order to once again learn... this time, to learn about someone else.

That same type of approach works with everyone, not just with a romantic partner. Asking questions helps us to connect with those around us because.

- We learn about others
- We subsequently learn about ourselves when we learn about others
- We demonstrate an interest in them (and people love to talk about themselves, so your questions show that you want to hear more about the topic that people love to talk about)
- When we demonstrate an interest in others, that builds rapport with them

As you meet other people, ask them questions. Ask questions of everyone:

- Prospective employees
- Current employees
- Prospective customers
- Current customers
- Past customers
- Vendors
- Family
- Friends
- … Even the people who serve you throughout your day, like the cashier at the grocery store or your dry cleaner!

So, what should ask them? Start with surface questions to learn their name and basic information about them. Then probe deeper with more penetrating questions (but remember to always be respectful!) about what is important to them in their life. When appropriate, ask about where they were born and grew up, what hobbies and interests they have, what targets they have in life, and what inspires them to get out of bed every day. Of course not all of these questions will be appropriate for every person in every situation but my point is to push beyond those surface questions like "what is your name?" to the deeper questions that help us to understand a person's motivation.

Succeed In Any Situation With Better Questions

As a business owner, you every minute of every day is an opportunity for you to ask better questions so you build a better business.

For example, at the end of the day, why not gather your employees together briefly to ask them to share with each other about what they learned today and what they can do better tomorrow. Or, periodically ask your employees for anonymous feedback about your company and about how you can serve them better.

And although I've mentioned better questions in the context of communication, I should also take the opportunity to point out that asking better questions of yourself – even though it's not a specific communication-improving strategy – can help you also grow your business. Take the time daily to ask yourself questions like "what can I do better?"

and "how can I serve others at a higher level?" because those answers will also help your business.

How To Ask Better Questions

To help you ask better questions, start with this exercise: Throughout the day, pay attention to the questions you currently ask. Chances are, you'll discover that they are very surface questions like you might ask someone you just met, "what's your name?" or you might ask your employee, "did you finish that job I asked you to finish?"

Later, reflect on how you might go deeper and ask the same question in a better way, or even ask better questions.

Make a list of questions to ask people and memorize it as a tool you can use whenever you're interacting with someone.

When you ask questions, aim to ask a question and then ask a follow-up question to add detail. That way, you force yourself to go slightly deeper every time you ask.

Practice asking better questions. When you're with family and friends – which is a great place to practice anything because they are much more forgiving and there are no long-term business consequences if you screw up – ask your family and friends better questions. Start with something like "what don't I know about you already?"

The better quality your questions, the more likely you are to discover the right answers and to grow your relationships and your business as a result.

Take Action!

___ Stop doing actions (Actions you currently do now but should stop doing)

_____

_____

__ Keep doing actions (Actions you currently do now and should keep doing)

_____

_____

__ Start doing actions (Actions you don't do now but should start doing)

_____

_____

__ Who will do new actions? (Assign the action to yourself or someone else)

_____

_____

__ By when? (When will these actions be complete?)

_____

_____

LASER-FOCUSED TACTIC #12: SERVING THROUGH COMMUNICATION

We tend to think of communication as a method by which we transfer information. When I know something and I want the other person to know it, I communicate with them.

While that is a primary purpose of communication, communication is also a way that we can serve others. In this chapter I'll explain how.

Serving With Information

I'll start with the obvious one – we can use communication to transmit information that serves others. It's a twist on what we already know about communication. But rather than thinking of our communication as a way for us to share our knowledge with someone else, we need to think of it as a way for us to serve others.

As experts in the home service industry, we know a lot about the systems that work within a house to warm or cool a house, to deliver clean water or remove unwanted waste, to provide power, and so on. For most of us, though, that knowledge remains technical and when we talk to a customer we share technical information.

But if you think of your communication as serving then you change how you communicate that information: all that technical data in your head actually becomes a way for you to help your customers live safer, healthier, more comfortable lives and to live in a house that they don't have to think about how they'll get drinking water or power.

That mindset transforms how you communicate. Rather than relating technical information to a customer that they won't find relevant or interesting, you can communicate helpful information to them that serves them and helps them to live safer, healthier lives.

Here are some examples:

- Rather than talking about the details of why something doesn't work, share with the customer some of the causes and solutions. A simple example might be: Instead of saying: "your circuit breaker keeps tripping because there are too many outlets on a single line. You need should add another circuit to the panel and split your outlets," consider something like, "it looks like you could use more outlets. I can help you with that"

- If your customer asks you to repair their plumbing, share tips with your customer about how to maintain clean lines with regular maintenance so they don't clog up.

Think about the information you share with your customers. Do you baffle them with technical information that they don't care about? Revisit what you say and create scripts that are focused on communicating information in a way to help them live better lives.

The expert can use communication to transmit information, or, the expert can use communication to serve customers.

(This is how I approach my magazine Home ServiceMAX. I see it as a form of communication that can serve readers like you.)

Serving With Questions

Communicating is not just about transferring information. It's also about learning. You can serve your customers by asking better questions (which I've discussed in another chapter in this book).

Asking questions serves your customer because it focuses your attention on them and the problem they're facing. And when you ask better questions, you can move beyond the problem itself to the impact of the problem in your customer's life – which allows you to serve them by solving the problem and eliminating the problem's impact.

Questions should elicit facts about the situation, of course, but questions should also elicit the customer's feelings and the impact that their problem has on their life.

It seems so obvious and yet it's so easy to forget when you're with a customer: questions help us to gain information and they demonstrate our interest in a customer.

Serving With The Words We Use

Our ability to serve through communication is largely impacted by the words we use. Our vocabulary demonstrates our goal for any conversation with have with employees and customers.

Changing the vocabulary you use with your team: The words you choose around your team sets the tone for how you expect business to be done. And even if you try to separate how you communicate with your employees versus how you communicate with customers, your employees might not be able to make that distinction.

- Do you make coarse jokes and use funny nicknames when communicating with your employees? By doing that, you're setting a specific tone about how you want to run your business. Unfortunately, this doesn't serve your employees, your customers, or you because it can limit your growth and it makes it harder for you to lead your employees when they see you as the buddy they joke around with.

- Do you get frustrated and speak angrily to your team? By doing that, you're setting a specific tone about how you want to run your business. Unfortunately, this creates a caustic work environment where employees become combative or become afraid to do anything.

Replace your negative words with positive, helpful, and supportive words.

Changing the vocabulary you use with your customers: Your communication choices will also impact customers. In subtle ways, your vocabulary will help to determine just how satisfied your customers are with your service and whether they'll call you the next time they need the service you provide.

Customers may be embarrassed to have an outsider come into their home to fix something that's broken (and perhaps even more embarrassed if they were the one who broke it) so customers may feel particularly vulnerable when you show up.

In every interaction with a customer, always choose words that are respectful, helpful, confident, non-judgmental, and understandable. Remember that they don't deal with these house systems in the same way you do, and they don't care how they work... They just want their home back to normal. So watch what you say and how you say it and help the customer feel like they are in good hands.

At the end of every interaction with a customer, audit the words you said to consider whether you were respectful.

Use words like:

- "How can I help you?"
- "What challenges are you facing?"
- "How does that make you feel?"
- "That's frustrating... But are you okay?"

- "May I review this with you?"
- "I'll take care of it for you – no problem!"
- "I'll do that right away."

Notice how these words are welcoming, confident, and respectful.

Communication is a tool to transmit information from one person to another but it's so much more. It's an opportunity to serve someone as well. By making small changes to what you say and how you say it, you can serve others at a higher level even through the way you communicate.

Take Action!

__ Stop doing actions (Actions you currently do now but should stop doing)

_____

_____

__ Keep doing actions (Actions you currently do now and should keep doing)

_____

_____

__ Start doing actions (Actions you don't do now but should start doing)

_____

_____

__ Who will do new actions? (Assign the action to yourself or someone else)

_____

_____

__ By when? (When will these actions be complete?)

_____

_____

LASER-FOCUSED TACTIC #13: HAVE A TARGET FOR EVERY INTERACTION

I've said throughout this book that the communication is complex. In spite of its complexity, every time you communicate, there are really only two outcomes that you will have – to get information or to change behavior.

- To get information (i.e. from a customer about what challenges they are facing with the problem they called you about)
- To change behavior (i.e. to get your team to start doing something, change what they are doing, or stop doing something)

Let me illustrate with a very simple example: Sitting around the dinner table with your family is an interaction allows you to gain information (like asking your children, "how was your day at school?") or to change before (like telling your children, "you need to ask for someone to pass you the salad – don't just reach across the table.")

The same is true in every work communication with your team and with customers. For example, you communicate to gain information or to change behavior. You tell your team something to share a piece of information with them, or you send out an email with a new process that you want them to follow, which is a behavior change. Even telling a customer the price of the service you just performed is a communication to compel them to pay.

Communication is complex but there are really only two outcomes for every interaction. With that in mind, I want to elevate your communication by showing you how to take a more strategic approach: have a specific target you want to achieve in every interaction.

That means: every interaction you have – whether spoken or written – should have one specific result you intend to accomplish… Either to get more information or to change a specific behavior.

This is true if you're talking face-to-face with a customer, sending out an email to your team, having a meeting, or enjoying a dinner with your family!

Even though this is true, and you might even be saying "I can figure that out for myself," most people miss the opportunity to think intentionally and strategically about how each communication will do one of those two things. Instead, they just communicate and get the information or try to

75

change behaviors but that result is an implicit (hidden and unstated) expectation.

But what if you were clearer, more intentional, and strategic? Rather than letting that information-getting or behavior-changing communication "just happen", what if you intentionally set out to achieve that result?

Before you have any communication, think carefully about what you want to accomplish.

For example, to get information you might think, "I want to know what challenges my customer is facing because their furnace isn't working," or, "I want to hear at least one great idea from each of my employees about how we can serve our market more effectively."

Or, for example, to change behavior you might think, "I want to help my employees do a better job of greeting each customer when they arrive at the customer's house," or, "I want my customer to recommend my business to family and friends."

By intentionally stating your desired outcome to yourself first, you will do a number of things:

- You will have time to review your desired target for the communication and determine whether it's what you actually need
- You will clarify your thinking about what needs to be said and what doesn't
- You will have time to choose the best words to say
- You will be able to reduce or eliminate any non-essential or distracting elements that are not necessary
- You will more clearly articulate what you expect from people and increase the likelihood that you will get that information or that behavior change

This small change to the way you communicate has the potential to transform every conversation you have... Even the "shooting the shit" conversations that you might have when you bump into someone on a Friday afternoon when you each have two minutes to talk about what you're doing on the weekend. When you intentionally determine to either get information or change a behavior, you'll approach the conversation very differently: Your casual conversation with the employee becomes not just an opportunity for the two of you to waste a couple of minutes in idle chitchat but it's an opportunity for you to learn about your employee and how they like to spend their time... and that information may be valuable for you to help you serve them better.

All communication has just two outcomes. Be intentional in how you approach your communication and you'll communicate more effectively and get more out of every interaction.

Take Action!

__ Stop doing actions (Actions you currently do now but should stop doing)

_____

_____

__ Keep doing actions (Actions you currently do now and should keep doing)

_____

_____

__ Start doing actions (Actions you don't do now but should start doing)

_____

_____

__ Who will do new actions? (Assign the action to yourself or someone else)

_____

_____

___ By when? (When will these actions be complete?)

_____

_____

LASER-FOCUSED TACTIC #14: WHAT TO DO WHEN COMMUNICATION TURNS INTO CONFLICT

Everyone has their own thoughts and opinions about things, and those opinions don't always align with the thoughts and opinions of others around them. You may encounter a situation on your team when communication turns to conflict because opinions aren't aligned.

Conflicts will arise in the workplace – it's inevitable. However, you need to remember that conflict is not necessarily a bad thing. Unfortunately, most of us try to avoid conflict as much as we can because we see it as negative. And certainly there are times when it can be (such as when tempers flare or when the conflict occurs between team members in front of a customer).

And while conflict can sometimes feel uncomfortable, it can be healthy and productive and very positive for the business.

Unfortunately, many business owners incorrectly assume that all conflict is bad so they do whatever they can to avoid it, and ultimately create an environment that is unhealthy and unproductive. Most failures in business and in relationships is the result of poor communication, and more specifically from not being able to handle conflict correctly (either by over-reacting or ignoring it completely). Good communication happens when people have trust and rapport with each other and feel that they can safely communicate – and even disagree.

Meaningful conflict can help create a successful business. This surprises most people but we see it is true everywhere we look: even in nature, broken bones grow back stronger, forest fires help clear out the deadwood to make room for new growth, and only the strong animals that survive conflict survive.

In business, similar benefits apply: disagreements are necessary for problem solving and for strengthening relationships. When people are free to disagree, it is more likely that all options for a project will be discussed and that better decisions will be made.

Before any conflict occurs in your business, the best approach is to always set expectations and foster an environment of respect among the team. Tell your team that conflict is okay when communicated appropriately. Set expectations about what healthy conflict looks like and encourage your team to have regular conversations even if there is friendly and professional disagreement.

Appoint a conflict manager in your organization – someone who helps people get past the more challenging conflict that escalates beyond professional disagreement. In my company, we instituted a "stop word" or "safe word" that was used if conflict was starting to get out of hand. We used the word "bamboo." Whenever there was a meeting and the discussion started to get heated, someone only had to say the word "bamboo" and we would stop the meeting completely and reconvene later when everyone had a chance to cool down and think about the discussion. It's a very powerful practice to keep meetings from getting out of hand. Institute a similar practice in your company and use it whether it's a meeting between two people or the entire company.

Recognize employees who are willing to go against the flow and voice a differing opinion. Thank them for taking a stand. However, make sure that your employees are able to support their recommendations with facts and figures. Disagreeing just to disagree will get you nowhere and personal attacks are never acceptable.

What To Do When Conflict Arises In Your Business

When conflict does arise, ensure that both parties get the opportunity to share their opinions and are heard. Conflict becomes unhealthy when someone wins only because they were louder than the person they disagreed with.

Encourage team members to back up their ideas and opinions with facts as much as possible. This might not always be possible (the conflict could be about opinions on how things might work and both could be speculative instead of fact based) but facts are helpful.

Educate your team to understand that conflict does not always have to be resolved right away. Conflict occurs when opinions and thoughts are not aligned and, in many cases, business can continue and the customer can still be served even if a few peoples' opinions are not fully aligned. As long as the misalignment is not impacting customer service or the healthy operation of the business, the conflict can raise questions and ideas that can be considered by decision-makers.

Be prepared as a leader to step in if necessary to moderate the discussion, especially if you sense that tempers are getting out of control. Your job isn't always to choose one over the other (sometimes you will need to if it has to do with how your employees serve customers) but often your job will simply be to ensure that the conflict remains as a healthy and productive discussion.

If you experience little dissension in your workplace, look at your own attitudes and actions. Do you send verbal or nonverbal messages that suggest disagreement will not be tolerated? Do you "grill" employees publicly when they suggest completion of a task via different methods than you had originally proposed? Do you punish employees when a solution they had proposed to a problem fails? Discuss with your employees if and why they are reluctant to voice differing opinions. Rectify any problems, including your own attitudes, which may be standing in the way of healthy, constructive work conflict and debate.

Take a look at your business and the culture you've established. Does it encourage conflict? No conflict at all is a warning sign that something is wrong in your company, as is too much conflict or conflict that becomes unproductive and emotional. Somewhere in the middle of those two extremes is where your company needs to be – actively encouraging healthy conflict to ensure that everyone's ideas are shared.

Take Action!

__ Stop doing actions (Actions you currently do now but should stop doing)

_____

_____

__ Keep doing actions (Actions you currently do now and should keep doing)

_____

_____

__ Start doing actions (Actions you don't do now but should start doing)

_____

_____

__ Who will do new actions? (Assign the action to yourself or someone else)

_____

_____

__ By when? (When will these actions be complete?)

_____

_____

LASER-FOCUSED TACTIC #15: NOT ALL COMMUNICATION IS ROSES AND RAINBOWS

Leaders don't always deal with happy news. Sometimes, they have to deal with the challenging aspects of a business and that may mean communicating about something negative or delivering bad news.

Perhaps you need to reprimand an employee as part of your employee feedback. Perhaps you need to let an employee go from your company. Perhaps even there is bad news to deliver to a customer, such as they will need to replace the furnace that they were hoping could just be repaired.

In this chapter I'll share with you some strategies to deliver this difficult, sometimes negative information effectively.

No one wants to share bad news or hear bad news but sometimes it's necessary and it's an important part of communication and as a leader it's part of your job to deliver the bad news and to ensure that your team can also effectively deliver bad news when necessary.

I always say "a shit sandwich is exactly what it is." What I mean by that is: it's okay to communicate bad news to someone when necessary but do so in a matter that is productive and respectful. Don't ever communicate negative information to someone to lessen them.

For example, even something as seemingly negative as letting someone go from your company can be done professionally and with respect in a way that elevates them because you're helping to remove them from your company, which isn't aligned with them and giving them the opportunity to find a job that does align with them.

It's necessary to deliver bad news sometimes but do so professionally, respectfully, and never to diminish the other person.

Here are some strategies to do so effectively:

Don't procrastinate. The longer you leave this communication, the worse the situation might get. In the case of reprimanding an employee, for example, you need to address the unwanted behavior right away while it is still fresh. Eliminate procrastination and accept your role as the leader to step up and deliver whatever news is necessary whenever it is necessary.

Be serious. It's very tempting to try and lighten the mood, perhaps with a joke or trying to put a positive spin on a difficult situation. Don't do that. Be serious. That doesn't mean you have to be grave or melancholy about your delivery, but it does mean matching the seriousness of your delivery to the seriousness of the news.

Be private. Only share bad news with those who need to hear it. In some cases, such as the case of reprimanding an employee or letting an employee go, that conversation should only take place with the employee themselves and possibly with a Human Resources (HR) staff member present. If you need to deliver some bad news about the company performance – for example, if there is a financial concern – that only needs to be shared among the executives and not with every employee.

Get to the point right away. Our natural inclination is to avoid bad news and it can mean we procrastinate in even delivering it at all and then, when we're face-to-face with the person we're talking to, we can avoid it further with small talk. Don't beat around the bush – get right to it right away. Be direct.

When possible, offer solutions. Sometimes you need to deliver the negative information to someone else because it's their job to come up with a solution (and that's certainly the case when you reprimand employees, for example). However, as much as possible, offer solutions or at least be prepared to discuss a way forward. Note: a solution doesn't always mean a choice:

- If you're talking to customers about the condition of their furnace, you'll definitely want to have at least one solution available them and you can allow them to choose from some of your recommendations.
- If you're talking to an employee because you're letting them go, there isn't really a choice but you are presenting them with a way forward.

When possible, use facts. Some bad news can seem even more negative if the listener doesn't understand how the situation came to be like that. You should always arm yourself with facts and documentation. It won't always be possible but do so as much as you can. If the bad news you're delivering is to let an employee go then make sure you have their employee file with the documented reasons why they are leaving. If the bad news you're delivering is to a customer because their furnace needs to be replaced then make sure you have facts about what is wrong with their furnace (which will assure them that your assessment is accurate and you're not just trying to sell them a more expensive replacement).

Always approach the communication as an opportunity to serve. This might sound strange because we tend to think of bad news as the opposite of serving but it is possible to serve while talking about a negative situation.

- An employee reprimand is serving your employee because you're giving them feedback about how they continue working for your company at the level you expect. (Plus, you're also serving your other employees and your customers by raising that employee to the level they need to be at).
- Letting an employee go is serving that employee because you're giving them an opportunity to find employment elsewhere that is more aligned with their values and vision for their lives. (Plus, you're also serving your other employees and your customers by ensuring your team is only made up of superstars who are aligned).
- Telling a customer that they need to replace their furnace serves them by helping them giving them the fastest, most practical solution to the problem they called you about.

Allow the other person time to process the information. Understand that some bad news may be emotionally impactful to the listener or may require them to think about it for a short period of time. Remember that you have probably had a little longer to process the information so don't expect them to "catch up" to your level familiarity and acceptance of the news. Deliver your news and then stop talking and allow them to process the information.

No one wants to deliver bad news but it is part of the leader's job. Fortunately, communicating about a negative situation doesn't have to be as difficult as you might think. Use the tips in this chapter to help you fulfill this part of your role as leader. And if you want to further build your knowledge of how to serve customers and how to deliver employee feedback and manage your team (all of which are key components of talking about negative situations) then check out my book *The Secrets Of Business Mastery*, where delve into these topics very deeply.

Take Action!

__ Stop doing actions (Actions you currently do now but should stop doing)

_____

_____

__ Keep doing actions (Actions you currently do now and should keep doing)

_____

_____

__ Start doing actions (Actions you don't do now but should start doing)

_____

_____

__ Who will do new actions? (Assign the action to yourself or someone else)

_____

_____

__ By when? (When will these actions be complete?)

_____

_____

LASER-FOCUSED TACTIC #16: WORDS MATTER, REGARDLESS OF HOW THEY'RE SAID

Throughout this book I have been generally referring to communication as spoken, although I mentioned in the Introduction that I use this for consistency and most of the principles discussed in this book apply to both spoken and written communication.

In this chapter I want to explore the differences between the two to give you a framework for understanding when and how to use the most appropriate communication method.

Even the terms "spoken" and "written" communication are somewhat limiting, since recording a video has benefits and drawbacks from both spoken and written communication, and sending a text versus sending an email are two very different forms of communication.

Advantages And Disadvantages Of Spoken Communication

There are advantages and disadvantages of spoken communication.

Advantages:

- You can (usually) get visual feedback from your audience as you speak to them (or verbal feedback if you're speaking over the phone), which will allow you to alter your message if there is misunderstanding.
- This type of information is quick and your body language and the context in which you're communicating can help aid understanding.

Disadvantages:

- You can't take back your words. Once spoken, your words are out there and even a simple mistake can cause confusion. Sure, you might be able to correct yourself but sometimes the damage will already be done.
- If there is disagreement or questions, you might be expected to address them right away.

- Unless the spoken word is recorded, it is spoken and then "gone" so that there is no record of what has actually been said but rather the only thing that remains is what everyone interprets was said.

There are advantages and disadvantages of written communication.

Advantages:
- You can take your time constructing your communication and you can go back and revise and edit before sending.
- Written communication has a record, a "paper trail" and a sense of permanence (more so if it's in a document like an employee handbook; less so if it's in a text). This is advantageous if you want to refer to it again in the future or if there is a disagreement over what was said.

Disadvantages:
- Written communication has a record, a "paper trail" and a sense of permanence (more so if it's in a document like an employee handbook; less so if it's in a text).

There Are Many Ways To Communicate
So far in this book I've talked about the process and practice of communication. But now I want to talk about the method or media you'll use to communicate.

There are many different tools or media you can use to communicate with others. Of course face-to-face is the original form of communication and it's also the most effective because you can see and hear the other person so you hear their words as well as their tonality and you see their physiology, and all of that helps the communication process.

But there are other ways to communicate: For example, there's written word – from hand-written notes to typed documentation to emails. And there's spoken word – from a telephone conversation to a recorded message to a podcast.

The problem with written-only and spoken-only communication is that you are removed from the presence of the other person so you only get the words they are communicated but not necessarily the other components that help to influence your understanding. For example, you don't hear tonality in a written email (unless the person writes in all-caps and understands what that means in email etiquette). And in a phone call you might hear the words and tonality but you don't see their physiology so you miss out on one of the biggest pieces of communication.

Fortunately, there are tools to bridge the gap between you and your distant audience and allow you to hear and see them. Tools like Skype, Facetime, video conferencing, and even pre-recorded video will all help you to communicate as fully as you can even if you're not in the same room.

Which tool should you use? Consider the purpose of the communication. Here are some examples:

- If you need to communicate a single message to a large group of people who are scattered over a distance and might not all get your message at the same time, consider using a pre-recorded video or call broadcast.

- If you need to solicit feedback from everyone and you want to do it as efficiently as possible, consider bringing everyone in for a face-to-face meeting. If that's not possible, consider group conferencing software.

- If you have a short message that you need your team to know, consider something like an email or text broadcast.

- If you have a serious conversation to have with someone, a face-to-face meeting is probably the most appropriate.

These are just a few examples. There are many situations you'll face in your business and I can't predict them all or prescribe something for every situation. Besides, innovators are always coming out with new technology that can transform communication.

Rather, you need to consider what tools you have available, whether the message is long or short, how important it is that everyone gets it at the same time, whether it's a one-way message or you want interaction, and how complex the information is (and whether body language will help in understanding).

Nearly everything I've discussed in this book will be applicable, to some degree, in every communication method. Your job as a leader is to figure out what you need to communicate and then choose the tool that will allow you to communicate most effectively to the right people at the right time.

Take Action!

__ Stop doing actions (Actions you currently do now but should stop doing)

_____

_____

__ Keep doing actions (Actions you currently do now and should keep doing)

_____

_____

__ Start doing actions (Actions you don't do now but should start doing)

_____

_____

__ Who will do new actions? (Assign the action to yourself or someone else)

_____

_____

__ By when? (When will these actions be complete?)

_____

_____

LASER-FOCUSED TACTIC #17: WATCH FOR HIDDEN SIGNALS

Our world would be totally different if everyone just said what they thought.

In some ways it would be better because people would openly share their opinions and feelings and, as a business owner, you'd always know exactly what your customers were thinking and how you can improve your service for them.

But, in some ways it would be worse: there is also value in a society that is polite and respectful, and sometimes it's appropriate to say something polite rather than to say what you're really thinking.

Since we don't live in a world where we always speak exactly what's on our mind, we need to watch for hidden signals from our listeners to help us understand how we are communicating to them.

People give off signals all the time, even though they don't realize it, and those signals are a useful way for you to understand what they're thinking and whether they understand what you are communicating.

There are several signals that I'll cover here (although there are more signals beyond what I'm covering. I'll cover the most common ones).

Body Language

Watch for body language to tell you what they are thinking.

- The feet tell us a lot about what a person is thinking. Are their feet pointing in your general direction? Chances are they're engaged. Are their feet tapping? Chances are, they are impatient for the conversation to end.

- Watch how people use their arms. Are they open and relaxed? Chances are they are listening. Are they folded across the chest? Chances are they are resisting something you're saying.

- Look at their hands. Hands fidget when they are impatient and they clench when they're angry.

- The mouth is the most obvious part of the body to interpret body language – a smile or a frown can reveal a person's thoughts.

- Eyes (including eyebrows) will also reveal someone's thoughts: Squinting could mean thinking; squinting with lowered eyebrows could mean anger.

Be aware that these are just general guidelines and should be used in conjunction with other tools listed here. For example, someone might be folding their arms because they are cold, not resistant; or they might be squinting because they forgot their glasses; not angry. So use body language as a hint but consider other factors as well.

Changes In Language/Tone/Pace

Another powerful way to understand what someone is thinking is to listen for changes in the way they say things.

People who become angry or frustrated will have shorter, sharper sentences, their tone might deepen or raise, and their pace will pick up.

And, people who are happy will have a warmer and even "musical" tone, use more words, and deliver those words at a slightly slower pace.

People who are confused might ask more questions or might tend to repeat things you said.

Agreement And Restatement

One powerful way to watch for hidden signals is to watch for agreement and restatement. People who agree with you are generally going to be positive about your communication (although you should be aware that some cultures will agree even if they don't understand what you are saying).

And in particular, watch for people to restate what you said: when someone parrots back the information to you, that's a sign that they were listening, but when someone restates the information back to you in a way that is complete and accurate, that's a sign that they understood what you said and have applied it to them.

When the situation is appropriate, you may even invite someone to restate back to you what you just said as a way to check to see that they understood.

There's a flipside to this signal as well: If someone listens and doesn't indicate agreement, don't assume that they agree just because they didn't disagree. Some people don't like conflict so they'll just listen even if they disagree.

Also, watch for people who say "but" a lot or respond to every point you make with a problem or challenge. Chances are, they're not trying to be difficult or find a loophole – they likely disagree or don't understand.

Take Action!

__ Stop doing actions (Actions you currently do now but should stop doing)

_____

_____

__ Keep doing actions (Actions you currently do now and should keep doing)

_____

_____

__ Start doing actions (Actions you don't do now but should start doing)

_____

_____

__ Who will do new actions? (Assign the action to yourself or someone else)

_____

_____

__ By when? (When will these actions be complete?)

_____

_____

LASER-FOCUSED TACTIC #18: HOW TO MAKE YOUR COMMUNICATION MORE EFFECTIVE

As you've read throughout this book, communication can be spoken or written words and it is heavily influenced by a number of factors.

In this chapter I want to show you how to take your communication to the next level and give you four strategies that you can use while you communicate to help you get your point across even more effectively.

But before I do that, I want to address something extremely important: the ROI of communication. Communication is one of the most powerful investments you can make in yourself and in your business. When you invest the time and effort to communicate effectively, your team performs at a higher level, your customers trust you more, and you grow your business. And even better than that, when you invest the time and effort to *improve* your communication, you're getting leverage on an investment that already pays massive dividends in your business. So make sure you schedule time regularly to improve your communication skills and your team's communication skills, and practice this skill just like you'd practice any skill. You'll be amazed at how quickly an investment into communication improvement can transform your business and your life.

Now, here are four strategies to get your post across even more effectively.

Demonstrate To Reinforce Your Message

When people hear something, they encounter that information with one sense. But when you demonstrate, they encounter that information with another sense as well.

Demonstrating the information can help you to communicate the information more clearly and will also help your listener to retain the information.

For your employees, use demonstration to help train them. For example, if you are teaching them about how to talk to a customer, walk them through a specific interaction with a customer. Roleplaying is an example here, in which you and another expert demonstrate to your team how to talk to a customer.

Another way to use demonstration with employees is when you are training new employees and apprentices about how to do something. In my book *The Secrets Of Business Mastery*, I talk about a simple process I use in which I explain how something is done and then I demonstrate how to do it (and later I get them to do it and then I get them to teach me). But demonstration is a key component.

For your customers, demonstration is very important. For example, if you recommend that your customer change their furnace filter every 3 months, don't just tell them that they need to do it – demonstrate how it's done. Walk them through step-by-step how to change the filter.

The examples I've given have been for face-to-face communication but it works just as well with other types of communication. For example, if you want to demonstrate a concept to your team but they are on the road, record a short video and then send out an email that explains what you want them to know and then links to the video for a demonstration.

Have The Listener Take Action

Demonstration is good but action takes it even further. This is where the listener is asked to do something as a result of what they heard – but specifically to do so in an environment where they can apply what they heard without worrying about making a mistake.

A good example is roleplaying with your team. First you might demonstrate the communication between you and another expert who knows what to do, and then you ask for your listeners to now participate and take action to practice what they have learned.

When used carefully and respectfully, this is also a great way to help your customers. For example, have them try the process of changing their furnace filter while you are there, just to make sure that they have the process solidified in their mind.

Action is a powerful way to make your communication more effective, especially when that action is taken in a safe environment where mistakes can be spotted and corrected before applying the information in the field.

And remember: action that is done incorrectly means that something was misunderstood – either because the listener didn't hear you correctly or because there was something wrong with how you were communicating.

Practice Makes Perfect

We've all been communicating all our lives so it's easy to take our own communication abilities for granted. However, communication is a skill that can be learned and improved upon, so practice what you want to say before you say it.

The more important something is to your business, the more you should practice it before you share it with your listeners. For example, if you want to make a company-wide change in how you greet customers on the phone, practice your instructions to everyone before delivering those instructions. Better yet, practice those instructions with someone else listening so they can provide constructive feedback to help improve what you say.

Practicing, even on the small things topics, can help hone your communication skills and increase the likelihood that you'll be understood and your expectations will align with your outcomes.

Use Examples For Clarity

When we communicate information, we're communicating concepts. Concepts can be hard to communicate because they are… well… conceptual. They are open to interpretation.

One way to make your communication more effective is to make those concepts concrete by giving examples. Examples help to illustrate your point with a story, case study, or analogy. They connect the conceptual idea with something that is familiar and memorable.

- Use examples sparingly so that your communication doesn't become long-winded.

- Make sure your example applies directly to your point. Avoid the temptation to use a funny story because it's funny; stick to your point!

- Be sure to always point out when you are using an example (otherwise, listeners might think that your point only applies in that specific situation).

Note: Creating good examples – whether stories, case studies, or analogies, is a skill that can make your communication more effective so practice this skill!

The communication process is complex and it's easy to think you are sharing your ideas clearly and effectively but then to be surprised by an unexpected outcome. Use these tools to help you take your communication to the next level.

Take Action!

__ Stop doing actions (Actions you currently do now but should stop doing)

_____

_____

__ Keep doing actions (Actions you currently do now and should keep doing)

_____

_____

__ Start doing actions (Actions you don't do now but should start doing)

_____

_____

__ Who will do new actions? (Assign the action to yourself or someone else)

_____

_____

__ By when? (When will these actions be complete?)

_____

_____

NEXT STEPS

In this short action-focused book, you've learned 18 powerful keys to help you communicate more effectively with your team, your customers, and anyone else you interact with in your business (and even in your personal life). The better you communicate, the better you can find alignment between expectations and outcomes.

These steps are only the beginning. Use these tools daily in your business. Here are other steps you should do as well:

1. Bookmark CEOwarrior.com, read the blog, watch the videos, sign up for the weekly newsletter, and learn more about the events and the Warrior Circle.
2. Get my books from Amazon:
    - *The Secrets of Business Mastery* for the 12 areas of mastery that can transform your business in 90 days or less.
    - *Secrets of Leadership Mastery* for 22 powerful keys to unlock your team's potential and get greater results.
3. Get the audio CD of The Secrets of Business Mastery at CEOwarrior.com/sobmaudiocd.
4. Watch for an upcoming Warrior Fast Track Academy where you'll spend 4 days working through many powerful strategies to build exciting, profitable change in your business. Visit CEOwarrior.com/events for more information.
5. Bookmark my magazine for the home service industry, HomeServiceMaxMag.com, and read each issue cover-to-cover, making notes and implementing changes as you go. (And, be sure to like the Facebook page at Facebook.com/HomeServiceMaxMag).
6. Bookmark my podcast, CEOwarrior.com/podcast, and watch for each new episode to reveal powerful strategies to grow your home service business.
7. Visit CEOwarrior.com to connect with me on Facebook, Twitter, LinkedIn, YouTube, and other social media.

CASE STUDY

Check out this case study article that describes one of my clients and how their business changed after working with me.

Petri Plumbing: Elevating From Good To Great... And Looking For More

What's the next step when you have a well-running plumbing business? For one business owner who was thinking about retiring, the answer seemed obvious: Sell his good company now. But then he met Mike Agugliaro who showed him how to elevate his company further and grow it from good... to great.

The Petri family have been in the plumbing trade since 1906. Their firm evolved over the decades, as many do, starting out with a couple of locations, partnering and then splitting off, renaming as the tradelines changed.

Michael Petri, a fourth generation plumber, got into the business in the in 1980's. He appreciated the heritage of the company but was also looking at where the business could go. At the time, the company was primarily focused on residential service and repair. Working with his father and brother, Michael Petri expanded their tradelines and renamed the company Petri Mechanical. He also started doing larger scale construction plumbing and became a union company.

This path for growth seemed to be set for the Petri business until setbacks struck in the 1990's. Michael Petri's father passed away, and Michael and his brother re-evaluated their direction and decided to split the company. Michael would return the Petri business to its focus on residential service and repair once again.

He began rebuilding the company. It was a smart decision that paid off: "We did well," Petri reports, "we were profitable." Petri's plan was to continue on this path, enjoy the profitability, and perhaps run out the clock on his retirement.

100

Things seemed good… at least outwardly. Inwardly, Petri's tenure in the business was taking its toll: "I've been doing the same thing for so long," he said. "I've been coming to this same building for nearly 60 years. After a while, there's no excitement to it. I became complacent and frustrated because I didn't know where I was going to go from here." The company's good performance was no longer a source of inspiration and excitement. Should he just keep plodding through until retirement? Should he shut the business down?

Things changed, though, when his son made a career switch, coming "home" from a career on Wall Street. Petri says, "when my son decided to join the family company, I started thinking that I should make it better for him, to hand off a great company to the fifth generation."

In spring 2014, Michael Petri met Mike Agugliaro: "I found Mike online and started following him," Petri said. He admits that he was skeptical of what Mike's claims. "I've been in the business for so long, I was skeptical. We messaged back and forth for months."

Fortunately, Petri's due diligence revealed that Mike Agugliaro delivered the kind of value Petri was looking for: "I was listening to one of his weekly phone calls and I saw a lot of value in what he was doing and how he was presenting himself and I decided to go to one of his 4-day events."

Petri threw himself into the process of listening to Mike and learning from his insight: "I signed up for his whole Warrior Group before even going to Mike's 4-day event – I found that much value in talking to him."

What changed Michael Petri from skeptical to committed? "Mike went out of his way to return my calls and emails… even if they weren't really important questions. Mike and Rob really cared about what I did. I see Mike as someone to take me from good to great."

Mike Agugliaro not only delivered on insightful value but also reignited a spark in Michael Petri for his business. Petri says, "I was thinking of retiring in about five years. But one of the things Mike kept saying was 'why? Why do you need to retire? Why don't you just build an infrastructure that will allow you to own the business and run your business without ever retiring?' I was somewhat complacent about my business when I met Mike but Mike convinced me that I could grow the business from afar." Petri saw how he could elevate his business from good to great… to exciting.

As he worked with Mike Agugliaro over the past year, Michael Petri started making changes in his business, he began putting systems in place and changed the way he does business. "We were successful before and I was looking to ease myself out of the business. Today it's different," Petri reports.

The changes have been invigorating: Petri has created systems for his business like a new dispatch system that transformed the company's efficiency. Their marketing changed too: "we were an older business and our work was passed down from generation to generation so I was never into marketing who we were. When I met Mike I saw the value of marketing to existing companies. I never believed that I needed PR but I've got a ton of compliments about the way Heather and her team [of PR firm Ripley PR] have done PR. We rebranded our company-- it was exciting. We have a new logo, truck wraps, marketing, and a new website. It reinvigorated how I viewed my business."

And the results? Michael Petri has seen his company break free from its complacent stagnation and began a refreshing new ascendance: "I've increased sales since I've been with him. Sales are up 30% annually since I met him. Our profit margins are still up there."

What's Michael Petri's advice to other service industry professionals? "I recommend Mike to a lot of younger people. You need a mentor or coach to put everything into perspective about what you do. The majority of business owners in our line of work think of this as a job. Mike's big on limiting beliefs, there isn't a person who doesn't have limiting beliefs."

Michael Petri is excited for what the future holds. Not only does he have a new perspective and a rekindled flame for his business, he's excited to be able to hand it off to the next generation. "We run 4 to 5 trucks right now. My younger son Christopher could build that up to 8 to 9 trucks." And Michael Petri is confident knowing that the business he's handing off, thanks to Mike Agugliaro, is a great business.

Service business owners: Are you running your business? Or are you running on empty?

Many service business owners are shocked to discover that running a service business can be an exhausting, expensive struggle. But it doesn't have to be. You don't have to sacrifice your money, your health, and your time with family.

In *The Secrets of Business Mastery*, Business Ninja Mike Agugliaro reveals how you can take charge of your business, dominate your market, and achieve the kind of dramatic results that you've only dreamed of. You'll discover powerful secrets like:

- Mike's transformational approach to service (this is a game-changer) and how it brings in a flood of higher-paying customers.
- The exact step-by-step market domination strategies (and Mike's proprietary checklist) to massively increase the effectiveness of every marketing campaign.
- A surprising new way to approach your finances to make more money and put more profit in your pocket.
- His time-saving way to find the best employees, and the technologies he uses to empower his team.
- Plus hundreds of other proven strategies and actions to implement into your business immediately.

Mike will reveal his $23 million dollar (and growing) blueprint to transform your business and achieve wealth and freedom. He'll lay out, step-by-step, exactly what you need to do daily in 12 areas of your business to take it to the next level.

Learn more at CEOwarrior.com/masterybook

Unlock your team's potential and serve your employees at a higher level.

You might have started your business by yourself but now your business has grown. You have a team and they're looking to you for inspiration, guidance, and instruction. You might be knowledgeable in your tradeline but are you an expert in leading others? (You need to be! Your employees and customers are relying on your leadership.)

In *Secrets Of Leadership Mastery*, Mike Agugliaro reveals 22 powerful and indispensable keys that will help any owner or manager to step up, transform their leadership skills, and build a high-performance team. You'll discover powerful secrets like:

- Systems: the secret ingredient to fast-track growth.
- How to quickly align your team and get everyone moving forward
- How NOT to be like "a boss".
- Why you SHOULDN'T be your employees' friend (many owners make this mistake).
- How to give powerful feedback and performance reviews that actually inspire positive change.
- Mike's most powerful conflict resolution strategies (these are a game-changer for many leaders).
- How to remove employees professionally – at some point it may happen and Mike shows you exactly how to do it.
- Catastrophic leadership blunders that could cost you your business.

Mike reveals the same strategies that he relies on to lead his team as he grows his business rapidly and blazes a trail that his employees follow.

Learn more at CEOwarrior.com/leadershipbook

Listen to the Secrets of Business Mastery Podcast

Whether you're at your desk, in your car, or out for a walk, Mike Agugliaro's Secrets Of Business Mastery Podcast is the perfect companion.

Each week, Mike shares his best strategies with you on topics like leadership, business start-up, how to grow your business, how to stop over-paying your taxes, and many more topics that are immediately impactful to your service business. You'll also hear Mike interview A-list guests who share their insight as well.

If you've never heard Mike before, this is a great way to get a glimpse into how he thinks – you'll hear his signature "no-holds-barred" style as he shares proven raw and real strategies that he perfected in-the-trenches.

And if you're familiar with Mike, this is another great way to hear from him and apply his game-changing strategies in your business.

Every show is packed full of practical information and motivation for every service business owner. Subscribe to them, listen to them over and over – they're the perfect way to stay informed and motivated no matter where you are.

Download free episodes on iTunes and at CEOwarrior.com/podcast

Warrior Fast Track Academy

Are you tired of treading water – staying busy in your business but never really getting ahead? Are you ready to discover the most powerful strategies to create real change, growth, and market domination in your business?

Whether you're new and totally overwhelmed or you're a seasoned pro and looking for to reignite, The Warrior Fast Track Academy can show you how to get to the next level.

Warrior Fast Track Academy is my 4-day hands-on event where I guide you and a group of like-minded service business owners through the exact plan that I used to build a $23 million (and growing) business. I'll reveal the blueprint and who you how you can implement the same blueprint into **your** business, with all areas of mastery planned out and ready to be plugged in. You'll be motivated and inspired to lead positive, profitable change in your company and take your business to never-before-seen heights.

Business owners who have attended the Warrior Fast Track Academy have said it's "life changing" and gone on to build successful businesses all around the world.

If you want to take control of your business and your future, Warrior Fast Track Academy is THE event to make that happen. To see what others are saying about Warrior Fast Track Academy, and to pre-register for an upcoming event, go to CEOwarrior.com/events

Warrior Circle

Have you ever wished you had a "Warrior Family" that could simultaneously hold you accountable for growing beyond your best self – and at the same time support your quest to get there?

Congratulations, you're home! If you elect to join Warrior Circle, this is what we do.

During the upcoming year, we will revolutionize your business and your life together. The Warrior Circle is committed to simplicity and balance. Together, we'll blow your wealth, freedom and personal goals out of the water by focusing on massive business building and life strategies.

We will also support you as you incorporate the 5 Dimensions of Life and Business Mastery – **Belief, Relationships, Health, Wealth, and Freedom** – and help you design activities and surroundings to support an amazing life!

This program is designed for go-getters and people who are ready to make the commitment and take action to boost their business.

To learn more about the Warrior Circle, and to see if you qualify to participate in the Mastermind, get in touch at <u>CEOwarrior.com/contact</u> .

Read The Free Magazine Written For The Home Service Industry

Discover new information, insight, and industry-specific success stories in **Home ServiceMAX** – the free online magazine written for home service business owners.

Each issue of Home ServiceMAX is packed with practical tips and strategies that you can implement right away into your home service business. They're field-tested and written by experts and industry insiders.

Home ServiceMAX will help you improve your sales, marketing, finance, human resources and customer service. Keep it on hand as you develop best practices to meet your team's unique challenges.

Whether you're a plumber, electrician, carpenter, roofer, builder, painter or specialist in any other service industry trade, to survive you must also stand out as a business leader. We designed this magazine to help you achieve that goal.

Each easy-to-read issue is available online for free. Check out the articles and make sure you have a pen and paper in hand to write down all the actions you'll want to take when you're done each article.

Read the current issue and subscribe here: <u>HomeServiceMaxMag.com</u> .

ABOUT THE AUTHOR

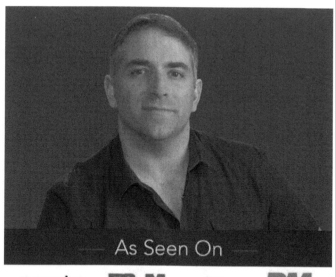

Mike Agugliaro helps his clients grow their service businesses utilizing his $23 Million Warrior Fast Track Academy Blueprint, which teaches them how to achieve massive wealth and market domination.

Two decades ago, he founded Gold Medal Electric with his business partner Rob. After nearly burning out, he and Rob made a change: they developed a powerful blueprint that grew the company. Today, Gold Medal Service is now the top service industry provider in Central New Jersey. With over 140 staff and 100 trucks on the road, Gold Medal Service now earns over $23 million in revenue each year.

Mike is a transformer who helps service business owners and other entrepreneurs master themselves and their businesses, take control of their dreams and choices, and accelerate their life and business growth to new heights. Mike is the author of the popular book *The Secrets Of Business Mastery*, in which he reveals 12 areas that all service business owners need to master.

Mike speaks and transforms around the world; his Warrior Fast Track Academy events are popular, transformational events for service business owners; he also leads a mastermind of business owners known as Warrior Circle. Mike has been featured in MSNBC, Financial Times, MoneyShow, CEO World, and more.

Mike is an avid martial artist who has studied karate, weaponry, jujitsu, and has even developed his own martial art and teaches it to others. The discipline of martial arts equips him to see and act on opportunities, create change in himself and others, and see that change through to successful completion.

Mike is a licensed electrician and electrical inspector, he is a certified Master Fire Walk Instructor, certified professional speaker, and a licensed practitioner of Neuro-Linguistic Programming (NLP).

Whether firewalking, breaking arrows on his neck, studying martial arts, transforming businesses, or running his own business, Mike Agugliaro leads by powerful example and is changing the lives and businesses of service business owners everywhere.

Mike lives in New Jersey with his wife and two children.

CONNECT WITH MIKE AGUGLIARO

Connect with me in the following places:

Website: **CEOwarrior.com**

Podcast: **CEOwarrior.com/podcast**

Events: **CEOwarrior.com/events**

Social: Visit **CEOwarrior.com** to connect with Mike on Facebook, Twitter, LinkedIn, and elsewhere.

Home ServiceMAX Magazine: **HomeServiceMaxMag.com**

Made in the USA
Middletown, DE
27 December 2015